CREATING WRITERS

CREATING WRITERS

LINKING ASSESSMENT AND WRITING INSTRUCTION

VICKI SPANDEL

RICHARD J. STIGGINS

Longman

New York & London

Creating Writers: Linking Assessment and Writing Instruction

Longman, 95 Church Street, White Plains, N.Y. 10601

Associated companies:
Longman Group Ltd., London
Longman Cheshire Pty., Melbourne
Longman Paul Pty., Auckland
Copp Clark Pitman, Toronto

This publication is based in part on work sponsored by the Office of
Educational Research and Improvement (OERI), U.S. Department of Education. The content does not necessarily reflect the views of the department or
any agency of the U.S. government.

Executive editor: Raymond T. O'Connell
Production editor: Linda Carbone
Text design: Lee Goldsteid
Cover design: Kevin C. Kall
Cover photo: Egyptian Travel Bureau
Production supervisor: Kathleen M. Ryan

Library of Congress Cataloging-in-Publication Data

Spandel, Vicki.
Creating writers: linking assessment and writing instruction/by Vicki Spandel,
    Richard J. Stiggins.
      p.   cm.
    ". . . based in part on work sponsored by the Office of Educational
Research and Improvement (OERI), U.S. Department of Education."
    Bibliography: p.
    Includes index.
    ISBN 0-8013-0055-X
    1. English language—Composition and exercises—Study and
teaching. 2. English language—Composition and exercises—Ability
testing. 3. English language—Rhetoric—Study and teaching.
4. English language—Rhetoric—Ability testing. 5. Grading and
marking (Students). I. Stiggins, Richard J. II. United States.
Office of Educational Research and Improvement. III. Title.
PE1404.S69 1990
808'.042'076--dc20   89-34263
                                                               CIP

ABCDEFGHIJ-ML-99 98 97 96 95 94 93 92 91 90

CONTENTS

Preface

Without high-quality assessment, it is not possible to diagnose the learning needs of individual students and student groups, to review the appropriateness of curriculum goals and content, to identify students for special services, or to evaluate the quality of teaching. In effective learning environments, assessment and instruction are inexorably linked.

Unfortunately, assessment and instruction are often seen as being at odds. Teachers sometimes view assessment as a necessary evil imposed on them by testing experts who have little sense of realities in the classroom. Often, they are right. For their part, assessment personnel tend to think that teachers are less concerned than they ought to be about achieving measurable outcomes. Sometimes, they too are right.

We believe that these long-standing perceptions are unproductive and unnecessary, since they result from an inappropriately narrow definition of *assessment*. As we shall show in this book, assessment need not be formal or "large-scale," and it need not be taken out of teachers' hands. Teachers can be in control of assessing their own students' performance, but controlling assessment well requires knowledge of procedures, as well as an understanding of the nature of assessment itself.

Assessment, as we've hinted, is more than large-scale testing or paper-and-pencil objective tests. Teachers who oppose testing are often reacting to once-a-year standardized testing during which someone from outside the classroom, school, or district sets educational priorities and objectives that seem arbitrary, then tests performance relating to those objectives. Teachers, seeing no real link between this version of assessment and the realities of the classroom, often conclude that assessment itself is irrelevant or, worse, intrusive. Few are inspired to seek in-depth training in assessment and evaluation.

In fact, many go out of their way to avoid such training. Who can blame them? As a result, these educators never have an opportunity to learn about assessment in a broader, more inclusive context or to acquire many of the strategies that could make their teaching easier and better.

The real irony is, of course, that such teachers do not abandon assessment. Far from it. They assess their students' work all the time. Often, however, they do not recognize that what they're doing *is assessment*, and, consequently, their assessment objectives and methods may be almost as arbitrary as those embodied in standardized testing. In order to be effective, classroom assessment must be systematic, must have purpose, and must be linked to instruction.

In this book, we hope to help teachers develop the skills and confidence that they need to put instruction and assessment back together in one critical area—writing. As a writing teacher and an expert in classroom assessment, we've combined our knowledge and classroom experience to show how writing assessment and instruction can work hand in hand to help students write better.

We concentrate our attention on classroom assessment and instruction, rather than on issues that are related to the currently popular large-scale writing assessments. However, it is our firm belief that many of the lessons of large-scale assessment have great potential benefits to the classroom teacher, and we propose to share some of what those lessons have taught us. Further, we focus our attention only on the direct assessment of writing proficiency, that is, on assessment via the evaluation of students' writing samples. Objective multiple-choice tests of language usage are addressed only in passing, for reasons that are outlined in the text.

Our primary audience is those who teach writing in language arts and other subjects. However, we acknowledge that those who support teachers' classroom efforts and those who specialize in educational measurement may also benefit from the ideas we present.

We have adopted a style that is informal and nontechnical, yet informative, we hope. We have included many anecdotes to help illustrate key points and from time to time we use personal pronouns (even first-person singular), because we find it comfortable to speak directly to the reader but less comfortable to say "we" all the time, even when we do agree. We think that our nontechnical approach sets this book apart from most textbooks on assessment. We hope it proves effective for you.

Our presentation begins in Chapter 1 with a discussion of the various roles that high-quality writing assessment can play in effective writing instruction. Chapter 2 describes and provides practice with two primary, direct writing-assessment scoring methods: holistic and analytical. Chapter 3 discusses these two scoring methods in terms of their advantages, disadvantages, and relationship to instruction.

Much attention is being paid these days to the need to teach writing as a process. In Chapter 4 we relate systematic writing assessment to the writing process by revealing where and how analytical feedback can help the learner to develop important process skills. In Chapter 5 we talk about the relationship between writing assessment results—grades—and effective instruction.

In Chapter 6, we urge that teachers take the risk of writing with their students, subjecting their own writing to assessment. In Chapters 7 and 8, we urge teachers to collaborate with one another to develop performance criteria, to assess student proficiency, and to teach the writing process.

Many people have contributed to the development of the ideas presented in these chapters. First, we'd like to acknowledge how much all of us in assessment owe to the thousands of student writers who, through their writings, have taught us so much. Not just the best of the writing, but *all* of the writing, has contributed in a very real way to our understanding of what writing is, what makes it work, and what makes it not work. It must be said that great numbers of these students, at all grade levels, have written with insight, perception, skill, and voice. Their writing has made us laugh, cry, think, forget about ourselves, and, perhaps best of all, know how lucky we are to be part of the teaching profession. To borrow a phrase from one student writer, these papers have truly "joyed my [our] day." Thanks particularly to Amy Lippert for her contribution of student perspectives.

We'd also like to express our deepest appreciation to Beaverton School District #48, Beaverton, Oregon, particularly to Carol Meyer, Evaluation Specialist, and to the many teachers from that district with whom it's been our pleasure to work over the past several years. Their professionalism and insistence upon making the district's writing assessment a true model for in-service have made it both delightful and educational for us to work with them. Truly, this has been among the finest experiences of our professional careers.

Special thanks also to the Analytical Writing Assessment Model Committee, a group of seventeen teachers (grades 3 through 12) from the Beaverton School District, who, in August 1984, worked with Vicki Spandel to design the original analytical scoring guide on which the one in this book is based.

In particular, we're indebted to Ronda Woodruff, a fourth-grade teacher at West Tualatin View Elementary School in the Beaverton school district, who so generously shared several documents that are reproduced in this text, as well as numerous stories about her successes in teaching writing and analytical assessment to students at the fourth- and sixth-grade levels. How fortunate her students are to have a teacher who so obviously looks forward to reading what they write.

We would like to express our thanks also to Wayne Neuburger, Assistant Superintendent, School Improvement, and Barbara Wolfe, Specialist, Language Arts, of the Oregon Department of Education, as well as writing assessment consultant Edys Quellmalz, for their encouragement and support over the past several years. Their concern for making state-level assessment a model for good classroom assessment has been a clear component of every project on which we've worked together and has given all of us an invaluable opportunity to discover what a powerful tool assessment can be in the hands of teachers who know how to use it wisely and well.

Our very deepest appreciation is given also to the members of the Analytical Scoring Team. Thank you for being wise, opinionated, caring, vociferous, adamant, humorous, insightful, provocative, droll, and so very, very good at your work. How much we've learned together, and (shall we let the secret out?) what *incredible* fun it's been.

On the off chance that persons who don't expect to be mentioned read acknowledgments, Vicki would also like to thank Margery Stricker Durham, a professor of English at the University of Minnesota, whose extremely close and thoughtful readings of her students' work and whose extensive comments and unanticipated questions showed how much it means to have a teacher who reads and thinks about what students write.

Further, we would like to thank those many teachers who have acknowledged that sound classroom assessment and thorough assessment training are, in fact, critical to them and to the well-being of their students. These teachers provide the energy that fuels their students, of whom we are two.

Finally, we would like to express our thanks to Sharon Lippert, who typed and retyped and retyped this manuscript and who had the graciousness to assess our early drafts only through her facial expressions. There's no doubt about it: It's much easier to revise with reckless abandon if you know that you have a talented support staff waiting to contribute to your work. Thank you very much, Sharon.

CREATING WRITERS

LINKING WRITING ASSESSMENT AND INSTRUCTION

■■ *Never hug a koala that hasn't been declawed.*

■■ *They were sop and wet.*

■■ *The police put out a search team for the sky and ground.*

■■ *The man was rapped in a large sum of clothing.*

■■ *It was hellishly odd!*

■■ *My father is quite an adventurer for 41.*

■■ *You shouldn't judge someone by its cover.*

■■ *Once a pond a time. . . .*

■■ *Even the governor should use friendship.*

■■ *Memories — you can never forget them.*

■■ *The last I saw of Boris was when he became a fur coat for a place called K-Mart.*

■■ *It was around 3 or 4 p.m., 1977.*

■■ *My spelling is abizmall.*

■■ *I had clusterphobia.*

The excerpts from the writing of elementary, junior high, and high school students that begin each chapter reflect the humor, wisdom, uncertainty, and insight so common to student writing on its way to "becoming."

■ SCENARIO

Ed and Ruth teach in the language arts department at the local high school. This is Ruth's first year at the high school. It's Ed's tenth year. Both are redesigning their lesson plans to accommodate the districtwide writing assessment that's scheduled for next week.

"What a pain," Ed remarks. "It wasn't so bad a couple of years ago when we were asked just to have the kids write on something and turn in the papers. Now that it's 'coordinated,' we have to take three days out of our schedule. The kids have to write on topics they're not interested in, and you know the worst part? We wait about six weeks to get the results back and find out that the average score in the district is 2.8 on a 4-point scale. Who cares?"

"But," Ruth interjects, "at least you have some support for what you've been saying—that kids have problems writing."

"Oh, come on," Ed retorts. "I don't need validation for that. You know it. I know it. *Everybody* knows it. What I don't know—and what this assessment won't tell me—is *why* they can't write. Until they can tell me that, I wish the testing people would just get out of my way and let me teach. I'll tell you something else, too. Some of these kids *can* write, and the district assessment isn't telling anybody about that, either. You know what I'd like? Something I could use in the classroom. The problem is, our writing assessment doesn't have anything to do with the way I teach writing."   ■

Ed has a good point. Too often writing assessment, as conducted by school districts or even by state departments of education, has little to do with writing instruction. Unless we can change this, it's difficult to justify the existence of these large-scale assessments. So, can we? In essence, this is what our book is all about.

Perhaps we should begin by saying something about what we mean by "assessment." For our purposes, writing assessment may be defined broadly as "taking a closer look at students' writing." Sounds simple maybe, but this closer look takes some thought if we are to do it well. Through effective assessment we can learn to uncover the strengths and weaknesses in students' writing. Then when we're asked what it is about Bill's (or Amy's or Don's or anyone's) writing that makes it succeed, we have a clear answer.

As we're identifying students' strengths and weaknesses, we, as teachers, are also learning what writing is, and sometimes we find that it isn't quite what we thought. Further, as we look at writing over time, we may find our definition shifting. We may start out, for instance, believing that correctness is what we'd like to see, but as we review what Bill has written, we find that it isn't strategically placed semicolons that bind us to the page. It's the insight, the telling sorts of details that only Bill could have recounted in just that way, the personal voice that makes us laugh or cry or say within ourselves, "Yes! Bill, you've nailed it. That's just the way life is, all right!" We read to learn about life and about ourselves. We write for the same reasons.

Of course, as we've hinted already, assessment is more than just reading through a piece of writing, although good analytical reading skills are the heart of good writing assessment. Skimming the text and reading for general impressions is risky. It's fine for reading in the backyard or at the beach; it's far less workable in the classroom where we're accountable for sharing our impressions with others and for using those impressions in helping ourselves and others to write more effectively.

Good assessment demands specific, clearly identified criteria. We have to know what it is we're looking for. If we start looking for different things next week or next year, we need to make note of this change and to let our criteria reflect this revision in values. As we become skilled at defining what it is we're looking for, we can share this secret with our students, and then we will have empowered them as critics of their own work—something every writer must be.

THE LINK BETWEEN LARGE-SCALE AND CLASSROOM ASSESSMENT

Perhaps it seems logical to assume that we would have learned to assess students' writing in the classroom and then translated what we had learned about classroom assessment into something large-scale, say, at the district or state level. This is sort of how it happened, but not quite. In reality, the evolution has been something like this: large-scale districtwide and statewide standardized assessments focused for a long while on either those elements of a formal essay style or on "correct" writing that could be measured through multiple-choice tests. More recently, large-scale assessment has attempted to take the best of what teachers know about assessing writing in the classroom and has systematized it in order to move away from multiple-choice tests and toward the direct assessment of writing proficiency via the evaluation of student writing samples.

In striving for consistency and efficiency, large-scale assessment has had to make some compromises. The classroom teacher who evaluates students' writing may spend five or ten minutes or more on a single paper, making marks on the copy, writing notes in the margins, adding a personal comment (and often a grade) at the end. In large-scale assessment, none of this can be allowed because the time required would make the assessment too costly. After all, some statewide or districtwide writing assessments include tens of thousands of student papers to be evaluated. Readers, who are also called raters, zip through the papers at a rate of one every two or three minutes (sometimes faster), make no marks on the copy at all, and add no marginal notes. They sum up their impressions on each paper by means of a score or a set of scores and move quickly to the next paper.

What we've discovered, however, is that these judgments—subjective and rapid though they are—can be, if the raters have been given good training and practice, remarkably reliable and valid. Furthermore, if the raters are using sound, thorough written criteria in assessing the papers, the quality and consistency of the feedback to the student writers far exceed what the classroom teacher, who is working in isolation, can usually provide. However, the best news is that teachers can benefit by applying some of this methodology in their classrooms.

Teachers typically don't care unduly about the averages that come from large-scale tests. This is because teachers know that averages often mask the realities—both the problems and the strengths—of real-life student performance. They do care, however, about the individual student's writing that has resulted in those averages. They care about the traits that characterize strong writing, about the kinds of problems that repeatedly emerge in weak writing, about which kinds of topics work and why, and about whether it's possible to assess writing rapidly and still give feedback that will help students become better writers. As it turns out, these are just the sorts of issues that large-scale writing assessment is helping us address.

So, we might say that large-scale writing assessment performs several services. It keeps writing in the public eye, reminding everyone of its importance in education. It provides data for those who need and want it. And it offers answers to some critical questions for those of us whose primary interest in assessment is the more selfish and personal desire to become better teachers of writing.

WAYS OF FORMALLY ASSESSING WRITING

There are traditionally two primary ways of assessing, or measuring, writing skill. These are *direct* and *indirect* assessment. Let's explore the direct method first.

Direct assessment requires that students actually produce a piece of writing: a story, a poem, an essay, a persuasive letter, or whatever. The rater then reads the writing and, by applying prespecified scoring criteria, judges the level of proficiency demonstrated and assigns a score (or a set of scores) to the writing, which reflects its place on a performance continuum.

The direct approach to assessing writing is not new. The Chinese started the practice thousands of years ago in order to identify promising young civil servants (DuBois, 1970), and it's been used in the United States for decades in college entrance examinations and as part of a procedure for screening prospective job applicants. Teachers tend to applaud this approach because it "feels right." If you want to find out whether someone can drive a car, you might give the person a multiple-choice quiz on the rules of the road, but, if this person is going to chauffeur you around, probably you would feel more comfortable if you took the person out on the freeway to see whether he or she could actually handle a car in traffic. Similarly, many people feel that the best way to find out whether students can write is to hand them pencils and paper and to ask them to produce something.

Writing samples are used widely at state and district levels to measure students' writing performance on a large-scale basis. There's scarcely a state in the country now that does not conduct some form of direct writing assessment, and, of course, direct assessment is used more informally at the classroom level all the time.

FORMS OF DIRECT ASSESSMENT

There are several popular forms of direct assessment commonly used at the district or state level, each defined according to the way in which the writing samples are scored. The three most common are *primary trait, holistic,* and *analytical.* Let's examine each of them briefly. (We'll look at holistic and analytical scoring—the two methods most commonly used in district or state assessment—in more detail in Chapter 2).

Primary-Trait Scoring

Primary-trait scoring is based on the premise that all writing is done for an audience and that successful writing will have the desired effect upon the audience—mainly due to the impact of the primary, or most important, trait within that piece of writing. The primary trait varies from context to context, depending upon the audience and the purpose at hand. In other words, if I'm writing a how-to paper on putting together a bicycle, then perhaps organization is the primary trait for successful writing within that piece, because, unless the steps are well ordered, I won't put my bicycle together correctly. On the other hand, if I'm writing a letter to a state senator in which I'm asking her to do something about the rising crime rate, then perhaps persuasiveness is the most important trait.

Primary-trait scoring has not been used widely in district-level or state-level assessment. Many teachers of writing feel it's too limited in scope to provide all the feedback needed about students' writing. Further, both teachers and assessment specialists point out the inherent difficulty in scoring just one trait while at the same time attempting to ignore others. Raters who try to do this often wind up exasperated. They frequently make comments like this: "I couldn't *understand* the ideas because the spelling was so bad." They mentally rate the spelling, and, as one might expect, this mental rating too often finds its way into the score for content or for whatever trait they're supposed to be attending to.

There's a related, slightly more subtle, problem as well, which has to do with how traits are defined. Take the trait of *persuasiveness*, for example. What is that, anyway? Some would argue that it's really an umbrella term that comprises ideas, organization, voice, and a host of other characteristics. Even good spelling can be persuasive. What senator will readily disperse funds to a cause spearheaded by a manager who can't spell? Thus, in primary-trait scoring, one has to be extraordinarily careful not to overload one trait with innumerable hidden subcategories, all of which are really being scored simultaneously. It's tricky—for the raters who score the papers and for the trainer who prepares them to score.

On the other hand, primary-trait scoring has met with more approval at the classroom level, where many teachers use it to teach highly focused skills. A teacher who is helping students learn to write effective business letters, for instance, may find it useful to teach and to score something called *persuasiveness*, knowing full well that it may comprise several qualities that she has time to discuss with her students in detail.

Suppose, however, that a teacher wants to see how everything comes together in a piece of writing—not just the organization, not just the persuasiveness of the piece, but the whole works. That teacher might find holistic assessment more satisfying.

Holistic Scoring

Holistic scoring is based on the theory that the whole is more than the sum of its parts and that the most valid assessment of writing will consider how *all* components of writing—organization, voice, mechanics, and so forth—work in harmony to achieve an overall effect. Holistic scoring may or may not be linked to specific written criteria, but when it is, it's sometimes termed *focused holistic* scoring; when it is not, it's sometimes termed *general impression* scoring.

In the absence of specific written criteria, holistic scoring is essentially a rank ordering of papers, with the best performances in a given sample receiving the highest scores, and the weakest performances receiving the lowest scores. Focused holistic scoring adds a criterion-based component so that student writing samples are not only compared to one another but matched against a list of specified criteria and scored accordingly.

Holistic scoring is an efficient method of selecting students who show the most promise with respect to writing skills or of selecting those students who are most in need of special assistance. Thus, it's ideally suited to selection or placement decisions that can be made on the basis of an overall impression of writing proficiency.

Because each paper receives only one score, however, holistic assessment has limited effectiveness in diagnosing writing skills; that is, it does not tell us, specifically, why one paper receives a higher score than another except in the most general sense—*it is better written*. One paper that receives, say, a 3 on a 5-point rating scale might have very strong voice but weak mechanics, while another paper that receives a 3 might have excellent control of mechanics but no voice. Teachers who want general information on who is succeeding and who is not will find holistic scoring quite efficient in answering this question. Teachers who want to know specifically how success in writing is defined for each given paper may find analytical scoring more useful.

Analytical Scoring

Analytical scoring acknowledges the underlying premise of holistic scoring that the whole is, indeed, more than the sum of its parts, but it adds that if we're to teach students to write, we must find a way to define the components of good writing and to talk intelligently about them in a language that student writers can understand and use in revision. Analytical scoring, then, is an attempt to define the main traits or characteristics of writing (e.g., *ideas, organization*) and to specify criteria that describe each of these traits in terms of the relevant strengths and weaknesses that we are likely to see in real samples of student writing. Holistic and analytical scoring systems frequently consider very similar sorts of traits. However, a paper scored holistically receives one score only (regardless of how many traits raters may mentally consider), whereas a paper scored analytically receives multiple scores—one per trait. How many traits are scored? Anywhere from two to ten or more, depending on the system.

Analytical scoring systems are not all alike, and some systems that pose as analytical are really primary trait scoring systems in disguise. They contain only two or three traits—not really enough, most writing teachers would argue, to provide any comprehensive picture of writing skill. An analytical system, however, that comprises enough traits to offer a more comprehensive profile (say, five or six) but not so many traits that it's hard to distinguish among them, offers excellent diagnostic potential. Because each trait is scored separately, results reveal specifically how and why each piece of writing did or did not succeed. A student who would have received a *holistic* score of 2 or 3 may receive, on the same paper, *analytical* scores of 5 in voice, 4 in ideas, 3 in organization, 2 in sentence structure, and 1 in mechanics.

Again, let us emphasize that for some purposes, an overall holistic score is probably sufficient. A holistic score of 3 might say, for example,

"There are some writing problems here, but there are some strengths overall to balance out these problems." Separate analytical scores provide the same information while at the same time linking it to specific traits, so that the message gains precision: "This paper has powerful voice, but very little control of mechanics. Sentences lack fluency. The ideas are quite well focused and developed, but the organization needs work." This is the kind of information that teachers find useful in the classroom; this is where analytical scoring really shines.

Now that we've considered several approaches to *direct* assessment (up-close analysis of student writing), let's take a moment to define *indirect* writing assessment, with an eye toward making some comparisons.

INDIRECT ASSESSMENT

The indirect method of assessing writing does not require students to write. Instead, it asks them to respond to questions (usually multiple-choice questions) about bits and pieces of someone else's writing. Under the indirect method, the test taker has to determine, for instance, which of several sentences contains a misspelled word, which of several punctuation marks will best separate two independent clauses, or which of several options shows the best way to combine four choppy sentences into one graceful one. Typical questions might look something like this:

Read the following sentence:
A. My mother is always
 B. traveling to distent countries
 C. like Pakistan Thailand and India.
D. No errors
 1. Which line, if any, has a spelling error?
 2. Which line, if any, contains a punctuation error?

Admittedly, these tests are getting better—better in the sense that they are getting more sophisticated. The best tests challenge students to really think about what makes a piece of writing work and not just to spot arbitrary capitals or find misplaced commas. Instead of giving students isolated fragments of text (sometimes as short as a single phrase or a sentence), today's tests often take large, coherent chunks—even whole stories—that students can review paragraph by paragraph or line by line. This approach more closely approximates the way real-life writers and editors work. An item from such a test might look like this:

Evaluate the underlined phrase and select the best choice:

Thor Heyerdahl became famous for a unique sailing expedition, which he later described in *Kon-Tiki.* Having developed a theory that the original Polynesians had sailed or drifted to the South Sea Islands from South America, it then had to be tested.

    1. A. No change
        B. he set out to test it.
        C. it was decided that it must be tested.
        D. the theory was then to be tested.

There's nothing wrong with using these indirect testing approaches, so long as we keep in mind what these tests are measuring: some of the prerequisites of good writing, but not writing *per se.* The ability to *recognize* good text is not the same as the ability to *compose* good text.

DIRECT AND INDIRECT ASSESSMENT: HOW ARE THEY INTERRELATED?

Let's think a bit more about the differences between direct and indirect writing assessment. Direct assessment measures students' ability to use what they know in producing and shaping text and connecting ideas, whereas indirect assessment says, in effect, "Look, I'll lay some ingredients of writing out here before you, and you tell me which elements within this text are conventionally more acceptable than others." These are inherently very different sorts of tasks. One is not necessarily more important or more difficult or more admirable than another. They're just different.

Being a critic is not the same thing as being an actor, but an insightful critic needs some knowledge of the actor's craft. Similarly, proofreading, editing, and critical reading—the sorts of skills measured by indirect assessment—are not precisely the same thing as writing, though many editorial skills help provide a foundation for writing. Do skillful editors make better writers? Probably. On the other hand, gifted writers probably have an edge in editing well. The point is, however, that editing is a skill in its own right—as is writing. Thus, a test that measures a person's ability to edit is not necessarily a good test of the person's ability to write—any more than a writing test is a good measure of editing skills.

THE IMPORTANCE OF OBJECTIVITY

No matter what we measure, we want our assessments to be objective —fair and untainted by any form of bias. The direct and indirect approaches to writing assessment achieve objectivity in different ways.

Direct assessments measure students' skills (e.g., the ability to write in an organized way) along performance continuums (e.g., a high of 5 down to a low of 1) with scores subjectively assigned by teachers. Indirect assessments include items that are scored as right or wrong. No subjective judgment is required of the person who scores the test. Does this mean that indirect assessments, with their right-or-wrong approach, are better? Definitely not. It just means that the terms for defining and the methods for achieving objectivity are going to differ between the two approaches.

With direct assessment, objectivity depends on the specificity of the scoring criteria and the quality of the rater training. When the criteria are highly refined and very explicit, and when the raters are very thoroughly trained and feel confident in applying those criteria in a consistent manner, the whole process becomes more "objective."

With indirect assessment, on the other hand, objectivity depends on the quality of the test items. Clear, unambiguous items that relate directly to the skills being measured make a test more objective. If items are ambiguous, if they do not relate to what's being taught in the classroom, or if they do not really reflect what the test raters value about writing, then the test is not very objective.

Although a certain amount of "objectivity" is desirable, however, we must be cautious about taking the position that subjectivity is somehow inherently evil. If we take this position, we'll find ourselves forever seeking ways to look objective when we're not. Face it: Direct assessment is a subjective process. There's nothing wrong with subjectivity, though, if it's applied with consistency and intelligence. After all, lots of things in this world are rated subjectively, and yet we place a certain amount of faith in those judgments. Films, books, restaurants, and performers in the Olympics are all rated subjectively, but we trust and value those ratings when they are given by persons with the training, insight, or experience required to make the ratings meaningful. When decisions really count—as in the Olympics—the raters use explicit criteria and apply them in a consistent manner. This is "objective subjectivity," if you will. Subjectivity isn't something we ought to apologize for *if* it's based on experience and expertise. This is the key. We wouldn't want writing teachers to judge an Olympic skating competition, and we would not ask skaters to judge writing samples.

At the same time, our judgments must be, if not totally objective, at least defensible. If I say, "Emily's writing in this piece about quarter horses isn't very good. I just sense it. That's how it seems to me," not only is my judgment not objective, it isn't defensible either. It's precisely the sort of intuition-based approach that has made many teachers suspicious of writing assessment—and rightly so. But suppose I say, "Well, Emily spells well and punctuates correctly, but her paper lacks development and shifts in focus here . . . and here. Emily's voice shines through with this humorous anecdote on page 1 but fades on page 3 with these generalizations about the importance of animals in one's life. The transitions between paragraphs are weak, and she includes numerous irrelevant details that distract the reader from the main story line about what to look for in buying a quarter horse." Now we're getting somewhere. Emily (or anyone else for that matter) has a right to disagree with my judgment, but at least it's based on solid criteria that we can all understand and talk about.

CORRELATIONS BETWEEN DIRECT AND INDIRECT ASSESSMENT

One school of thought argues that since a reasonably strong correlation, or relationship, exists between performance on direct (writing sample) and indirect (multiple-choice) tests, and since the multiple-choice version is generally easier and cheaper to administer and to score, why not use indirect tests? Advocates can almost always find results of a local or a national study that will support this position (though many will not), and strained school budgets can make the argument pretty compelling.

There are, however, problems with this way of thinking. For one thing, the correlational analyses can be tricky and must be interpreted very cautiously, especially in this case. Why? Well, for one thing, multiple-choice tests, like the people who write them, are not all alike. Some multiple-choice tests are better written than others, and their content is not consistent from test to test. Some focus more heavily on spelling, some on mechanics, some on usage, and some on editing skills.

Direct writing assessments also differ a lot. The how's and why's of these differences are complex, but, to put things in a nutshell, every direct writing assessment is based on its own individual set of criteria for judging writing. Teachers in Miami may or may not be considering the same sorts of criteria that teachers in New York or Los Angeles find important. Further, the way in which raters are trained and the general philosophical approach advocated by the person who does the training probably has as much to do, in the long run, with the way that the scores are assigned as the criteria themselves. So you see, trying to sum up the overall "correlation" between direct and indirect assessments is a little like summing up the correlation between clouds and rain; the potential patterns are countless and forever shifting, depending on the particular combination of direct and indirect measures that we are using and the nature of each.

It's fairly simple to speculate how we *might* achieve a high correlation between results on two hypothetical measures of writing skill—one direct and one indirect. Let's say that we are using an indirect measure that focuses heavily on writing conventions and that also we are conducting a direct assessment in which the trainer asks us to consider mechanics carefully. In this case, a very high correlation between results should not come as any surprise. The real danger, however, is that such results might encourage us to say, "Aha—see? You *can* measure writing skills with a multiple-choice test," when in fact all we've really shown is that we can measure students' *skill in using writing mechanics* in different ways—directly or indirectly.

RAISING EXPECTATIONS

Not all teachers by any means view mechanical correctness as the be-all and end-all of good writing. They don't read Norman Mailer because he has an extraordinary way with the periodic sentence, and they don't cite Shakespeare as a master of the semicolon. One reason why mechanics have held sway as the significant indicator of quality writing is the pressure of public opinion or, perhaps more accurately, of what is perceived to be public opinion. Teachers believe that parents, business people, and the general public want and demand conventional correctness in students' writing.

We've all heard the story about unfortunate students who cannot fill out a business form or write a letter for a job application without excessive embarrassment to themselves and, by extension, to their teachers. In an effort to rescue these unfortunate students, whose plight has commanded more than a fair share of our attention, we have often allowed our expectations in other areas to slip, and we have emerged, ironically, with a somewhat weakened standard of good writing that teachers too often feel pressured to uphold. This is sad. Teachers themselves know better, but reeducating other audiences, including parents, takes extraordinary skill and courage.

Don't look to the media for much support, either. Read any summary of results of writing assessment—even at the national level—and what you will typically find held aloft as proof of students' declining writing skills is a pathetic little piece in which the writer struggles to spell, capitalize, and punctuate, barely grasping where one sentence ends and the next begins.

Now stop and think. Have you ever seen a mechanically flawless composition held up as an example of poor writing? Probably not. Why? Because when pressed to defend their judgment that today's students cannot write, those who assess students' writing generally fall back on what's obvious: They point to spelling errors, grammatical flaws, slipshod punctuation, lack of paragraphing, inconsistent capitalization. They feel safe in citing these examples, because scarcely anyone questions them. Yet mechanically flawless pieces sometimes are poorly written, too.

Do we really not care what students say as long as they punctuate and spell correctly? We should. Content-free fluff is not good writing. If conventional correctness does indeed come at the spit-and-polish stage of the writing process, we ought to ask ourselves what it is we're polishing. Assessment, if it works well, ought to provide us with some answers. When assessment is doing the job it should do, we can hold up a piece of writing that receives high scores and say—and *mean* it—"Here's an example of what teachers in our district consider good writing."

RESHAPING WRITING THROUGH ASSESSMENT

How can we use assessment more effectively in improving writing instruction? First, we have to rethink what it is we mean by writing skill. We need to ask ourselves what it is we really value in good writing and challenge ourselves to put those criteria in writing for everyone to see. We must look carefully also at what it is that good writers do when they write and when they assess what they've written, and then we must ask how much of this can be duplicated in the classroom.

Second, we must ask ourselves what our purpose is in assessing writing in the first place. Is it to figure out how many or which students have writing problems, or is it to define the nature of the problems themselves? The answer has major implications for how we go about assessing the writing. If we're screening students for placement into classes in which they can receive special help, for example, this calls for one sort of assessment. If we're interested in assigning end-of-year grades, then we have another purpose for assessment with its own set of expectations. If we're assessing writing in order to provide students feedback during the writing process when they can most benefit from that feedback (while there's still time to fix things), then we need an assessment approach that will serve this particular purpose.

MAKING ASSESSMENT AN EFFECTIVE PART OF THE WRITING PROCESS

Good assessment should be an integral part of the writing process—not an interference and not just an end-of-the-line step.

As we noted earlier, all writing teachers and all writers "assess" in some way all the time. It's the "how" that differs. Revising and editing are forms of assessment. What we commonly call peer editing or peer review is also a form of assessment; so is grading, commenting on a piece of student writing, or sharing writing by reading it aloud (the very inflections of the reader constitute a subtle form of assessment). Even as you read this book, you're assessing it in a very real sense, and what you do as a result of reading it—sharing it with a colleague, using the ideas found in it, or sticking it on a back shelf somewhere—constitutes an outcome of that assessment.

Assessment isn't necessarily formal, and it does not always result in some sort of statistical data analysis. So the question at the classroom level is not *whether* to assess—because the fact is that assessment in some form is going on all the time—but rather *how* to assess and how to make better, more consistent use of the results.

The answer to this question, we believe, rests in developing a system of classroom assessment that

Reflects specific, well-defined, consistently applied criteria

Provides student writers and teachers with better insights about what makes a piece of writing work

Reveals the strengths, as well as the weaknesses, in writing

Gives teachers some welcome clues about what (specifically) they can do to help students write better

Provides students (as well as teachers, parents, and others) a working vocabulary that they can use to talk about writing

We should make it clear that while we're going to talk primarily about assessment within the classroom, we'll be referring to large-scale assessment frequently because what we've learned over the past few years in reviewing thousands of student writing samples has implications for assessment at the classroom level.

In the chapters that follow, we'll

Show how assessment can be integrated into the writing process

Look at alternative approaches to the evaluation of writing performance

Share some thoughts on why teachers of writing need to write

Discuss the pros and cons of grading

Describe one analytical writing assessment model that has worked well at both district and classroom levels for thousands of teachers and their students

Suggest ways that teachers can develop and use their own criteria for assessing writing in the classroom with the assistance of student writers

WHAT'S IN THIS FOR WRITING TEACHERS?

How will all of these ideas help teachers? Evaluating student writing samples has always been a time-consuming task for teachers. They don't need more to do. They need something to make the process more efficient, so that they can have their students write more often, as research and their own instincts tell them they should. As it is, however, they do not have enough time to review 150 student papers several times per week. A good assessment system can make this paper load manageable. Now, *there's* a promise writing teachers have heard a dozen times before, but fifteen years' worth of direct experience with writing assessment—and the attendant pressures of staying within budget—guarantee that our promise isn't an empty one this time.

Assessors who are faced with scoring tens of thousands of student papers at one time have *had* to develop rapid, cost-effective scoring procedures. So the real question is, "Can such procedures—admittedly developed with an eye on efficiency—still yield useful information to students who need to know how to make their writing better?" The answer is yes, if the criteria for scoring are clear, well defined, and truly reflective of what classroom teachers value.

Just what sort of time savings are we talking about? With holistic scoring, we've discovered that one overall performance rating can be assigned reliably in less than one minute per one-page paper. Raters who are interested in the greater specificity afforded by analytical scoring have found that they can reliably assess most two- or three-page papers at the rate of one every three to four minutes. (A few experienced raters are able to score much faster than this.) The quality of the feedback depends, again, on the thoroughness of the scoring criteria.

Further, when teachers, parents, and students agree on a common vocabulary to use in talking about writing, communication becomes more efficient. Students don't feel pressured to "psych out" teachers in order to get high grades, and they are not confused by the fact that every teacher seems to be looking for something a little different. Suddenly, students know what grades mean, and so do parents.

Teachers who use written scoring guides to assess writing don't have to write lengthy comments all the time. They are free to do so, of course. A good scoring guide should be a tool for stretching and revising our thinking about writing, not for reducing and shrinking it. The point is, however, that students who have (and use) their own copies of the scoring guide know what the scores mean, so extensive comments become less critical.

Thus new criteria need to be developed to evaluate more complex forms of student learning, and these criteria need to become part of traditional testing programs (Langer and Applebee, 1987, 147).

In evaluating students' writing, many teachers, regardless of the general method they use, feel compelled to serve as private editors for their students. They diligently search out every error in every paper and sometimes even correct the errors. No wonder they get tired. A good writing assessment system bypasses all this editing. Students may be scored on their handling of conventions, but teachers are not compelled to *fix* the conventions any more than they're compelled to insert transitions, flesh out ideas, punch up the voice, or rework the organization. That's the student writers' job. Within a short time, students learn to assess their own work. Then they gain full ownership of and full power over their words. Meanwhile, teachers have time to teach.

Most important, a good writing assessment system helps teachers and student writers to think and talk about writing. More important than the scores or the grades that the teachers assign are the reasons underlying them. Good assessment always demands criteria that are developed with care, shared openly, and revised or tossed aside when they no longer fit the way we think.

GUESS WHAT? STUDENTS CAN WRITE

One of the best-kept secrets in this country is the fact that, contrary to what we're often told, many young people *can* write. In fact, some write very well. One of the reasons that we haven't known this is that although we've subscribed heartily to the theory that writing is thinking, we've been slow in developing a writing assessment approach that really values thinking skills. The prompts—or writing topics—that we administer to students are often overwritten, sometimes downright inane, and tend to suppress rather than to encourage thinking. Furthermore, the criteria that we use to evaluate the results frequently have little to do with the logical ordering of ideas or with the writer's ability to surprise and to delight the reader, to sense relationships, to foreshadow consequences, or to build to a climax, or even something as basic yet telling as the writer's skill in holding a reader's attention for more than a paragraph.

We can do better, but we'll have to give up cheering over correctly used semicolons and formulate an assessment process that shows real respect for student writers *as writers*. Our standards in the past have not been too stringent; they've been alarmingly limited. Conventional correctness is a shiny veneer covering a lot of faults. We've settled for it because it looks good, but our student writers are capable of more than providing shiny veneers. Also, we're capable of providing guidelines for more than sentence revision. Why are we so timid about our expectations? If we want to see real writing improvement, we must begin demanding it—of them and of ourselves.

The child whose usage has been made reasonably "correct" or standard, but whose sentences are flat, dull, and inexact, has not been taught good English usage (Pooley, 1974, 155).

2

PRACTICE SCORING

- Face it—you are either a failure or a successor.
- The truth is, I was afraid of crashing, not flying.
- Ches get alode of this. . . .
- Well, mideswell, I thought.
- His hair is brown and 52 years old.
- Their legs are small but thick with mussels.
- "Oh say can you see by the donserly light. . . ."
- I find great enjoyment in just letting my mind flow freely like jello in a vacuum cleaner.
- The game is survival of the fittest; be a Republican and win it.
- Feeling a thump and hearing a blood curdling scream, my car stopped immediately.
- Fear has many parts and will probably never be figured out, especially by a 15-year-old student.
- Mom decided to halve Dad. . . .
- My dreams seem unrememberable.
- Dad was sprightly maligning the police.
- All the information in this report has been exsperested by the writer, so this report has some knowledge to this report.

This chapter will give you a chance to try holistic and analytical scoring with some sample student papers. Once you've tried each scoring approach, you can compare them to each other and to any form of assessing or grading with which you are familiar. You can also begin to see how criterion-based assessment might fit within a larger instructional program in the classroom.

The papers in this chapter have been collected over a period of years from writing assessments across the country. Identifying information (names, locations, etc.) within most papers has been changed; otherwise the papers are exactly as the writers produced them.

Most of those presented are middle-school or junior high-school level papers. Most are second drafts; that is, they come from assessments that were structured in a way that allowed students to write a first draft, set it aside for a day, and then return to it to revise, edit, and rewrite the "final" copy. Of course, a second draft is usually not the equivalent of a final copy. But the drafts are sufficiently revised to allow us to illustrate the points we wish to make.

The first part of this chapter will provide you with practice scoring in holistic assessment, the second part, with practice in analytical assessment.

HOLISTIC ASSESSMENT

Remember that in holistic scoring, you give one score to indicate how well the paper as a whole works. For this practice session, you'll be scoring midlevel (junior high-school) papers on a 5-point scale, with 5 being the highest score and 1 being the lowest.

In response to a frequently answered question, let us clarify that there is no *zero* score. Zero, if it is used at all in assessment, is reserved as a code for special papers that for one reason or another cannot be scored. These include

Totally blank papers

Papers that are so short that scores really mean nothing (e.g., just one sentence)

Papers that are written totally or primarily in a language other than English (unless, of course, members of the rating team are fluent in the second language)

Papers that do not deal with the topic at hand in any way whatsoever but are merely an open letter to the assessment raters. Here's an example:

> If I were principal I would do absolutely nothing. The job of principal is a job put down by society and I would not conform to society's rules.

To control others is almost as barbaric as what you are doing to me! How can you judge a fellow human being? Merely reading this in the intention to "grade" me instead of just to read show and intensifies your stupidity!

I'd like to know how much they paid you to put down another creation of God!

This whole assignment or assessment or whatever you want to call it is infuriating, but I'm supposed to do it anyway and I don't really care about you or what "grade" you give me, as a matter of fact, I hope you die!

Well, here I go, off to write a stupid assessment to test my writing skills and those of the rest of the students at Smockley High School.

If I were principal I would live in a dorm and show off at the pool. I wouldn't be there to teach, I'd just want to get drunk! I would make sure the students could have access to any part of the school at any time of the day and I'd have open campus.

There, I hope your satisfied! You can put your "grade" on me now and mark me for the rest of my school years. You are a sadistic animal!

Leave me alone!

Illegible papers—papers that literally cannot be deciphered by anyone on the team. There are very few of these, since language arts teachers are extraordinary decoders. The most outstanding example of this occurred when a student, whimsically perhaps, wrote his final draft right over his first draft. Unfortunately—in this case—he did change the wording.

Sloppy handwriting per se does not make a paper *illegible*. Our procedure has always been to score any paper we can read, provided the paper is scorable in other respects, and to ignore handwriting. The papers in this chapter are all typed, so you won't need to be concerned during this practice session about this common cause of rating bias.

How to Score

In scoring the papers holistically, you should consider the following traits, but you should not score any of them individually:

Quality and completeness of ideas, including focus and clarity

Development of ideas—the use of supporting details, examples, or anecdotes

Organization, or the way details and events are woven together to create a theme, to bring home a point, or to tell a story

Voice, or the sense of the writer behind the words

Word choice, meaning the freshness and appropriateness of the words and phrases that the writer selects

Sentence structure and fluency, or the overall sound and rhythm of the word patterns

Conventions, including grammar and usage, punctuation, spelling, paragraphing, and capitalization

Consider how the paper works *as a whole.* How effective is it? Does it make its point, and does it hold your attention while doing so? Does it make you want to read more? Is there some sign that the student is involved in the writing and has a sense of ownership?

Anchor Papers A, B, and C

All the papers that you will score in this section are written at the junior high-school level. All are written in response to the prompt, "Write about a favorite object that is important to you." In assigning scores, you will use the following anchor papers (A, B, and C) as guides. The term "anchor" simply refers to the fact that these papers are held to be representative of scores at different levels; thus, they provide an "anchor point" for raters who may assign scores by comparing one student's performance to that of another.

These three papers are representative of papers at the high (5), middle (3), and low (1) score levels on our 5-point holistic scale. We won't tell you which is which (yet). You need to figure it out. After you read them, assign a 5 to the one you think is best, a 3 to the midlevel paper, and a 1 to what you consider the weakest performance. Then compare your ratings with those presented at the end of the papers.

PAPER A

This summer I went to new orleenes and I raced bicycles and won ten trophes all first of course. I went duck hunting to. And we got a real big Mallord. My uncle and I went to the board Walk and road all the rides it was OK. We also played miniture golf. He beat me every time we played. We went cutting wood and I earned 4 hundred dollars and I spent it on bicycle rims for my racing bike Well I was down South my uncles girlfriend left him and took all his stuff with her like the t.v. microwave, VCR, stuff like that and when my uncle got home and saw what she done he riped all the doors off the wall and broke almost every window in the house good thing she wasn't there when he drove up! Now he has got over her and bought new stuff. and even has a new girlfriend.

SCORE (5, 3 or 1): _____

PAPER B

From my travel adventures of lost luggage, rain, pollution and other exciting mishaps, one item has survived.

My address book, well, isn't an address book. My mother gave it to me from her trip to Japan. The lines of the paper go the "wrong way" because the Japanese write their language vertically. I guess it was supposed to be an autograph book or a memo pad for busy Japanese executives. Somehow, I got it.

Oriental, sun-faced flowers decorate the cover. The edges are tattered but, being the collecting bug that I am, it will probably last for a few more decades to come.

On the inside are small pockets like the ones you had in a "peachy" notebook in high school. Usually, these pockets have to be cleaned out about once a month because various small bits of useless paper that I seem to attract find their way in.

Despite its war-veteran look, inside there are shiny new addresses waiting to be put to use. Phone numbers and doodles decorate the outskirts of my pages. Some people call it garbage, I call it character.

I've tried my hand at journals and the traditional jr. high diary. But it seems that my address book holds more memories than any literature I could ever produce.

As I turn the pages back, so turn back the years. Guilt sometimes catches up with me as I note people I haven't written, like Maggie or Tom. Other times I just smile and reminise. Some addresses stump me for a face or instance where I met them.

Please don't get the impression that I'm so popular I forget people, dear reader, or that I'm sickly rich. Actually, the real picture of me is an impoverished student who's had a lot of lucky breaks of travel (and is a lousy bookkeeper at recording them).

Why don't I organize you ask? Once, I did try to begin a new, neat, pre-organized address book. After filling in each address very neatly and alphabetically in order, I put it in the back of my desk drawer so I would not mess it up. It still sits there, now five years out of date, and my tattered old addressbook lives on.

Faces and eras of my life are kept brilliant and alive in this crazily kept book.

My handwriting changes into the mature, illegible script. The dirt, coffee and rain stains have entered into the last couple pages I've started on. Even a few tear stains, perhaps from joy, perhaps from sorrow, add to the personality of my encyclopedia of people.

I've stuck a lot of those yellow stick-on pads in it, too. "Addresses with an uncertain future" I call them. Some are plucked and enter the ever-famous "file" basket, others are written as an eccentric ceremony with me promising myself to faithfully keep in touch.

Only a few pages remain. Then it will be on to another disorganized, yet cherished, book. Then again, maybe I'll just buy some more yellow stick-ons.

SCORE (5, 3 or 1): _____

PAPER C. SPOON COLLECTION

I have a gigantic and beautul collection of spoons that my great grandma started me on by giving me her collection about five years ago.

I have about 130 charming spoons from all over the world.

My favorite one is from Thailand. It reminds me of a beautiful and colorful peacock with its feathers spread out. It has a delicate blooming pattern on it made out of thin copper wire.

I have another spoon I like. It is from Norway. It has a small windmill on it that gracefully turns in a circul. My aunt got it for me when she was in Europe a cupple years ago.

I keep my collection in my disastrous room.

I plan to keep the collection as long as I can, then give it to someone who will appreciate it and take good care of it.

SCORE (5, 3 or 1): _____

Suggested Scores for Anchor Papers (A, B, C)

Paper A: 1
Paper B: 5
Paper C: 3

Paper A is, of course, the weakest conventionally. In addition, however, it lacks focus. It's a scattered list of details that really never develops any central theme. It starts and stops haphazardly. It contains a hint of voice, which is not strong but is not absent either. The writer doesn't seem indifferent, exactly; he simply doesn't seem to have very much to say today. Despite an apparent wealth of material (in the hands of Larry McMurtry, this little episode could have become a novel), he's still fishing, and when the requisite two paragraphs' worth of space are filled, he wanders off to more interesting endeavors.

Now let's consider Paper B, which is the strongest of the three. ". . . my encyclopedia of people" has a nice ring to it. I like this piece very much. It has focus, it is well developed, and is real. Who of us can't identify, in some way, with this writer's topic? She has chosen something simple, but she has a lot to say. Her comments transcend address books and housekeeping habits. This is a paper about personal history. We're told about a book, but of course we're really learning about the writer and about ourselves.

If I were editing this paper, there are bits and pieces that I would change, but I remind myself that then it would be mine. This piece is very much this writer's own, and I respect and admire her easy phrasing. Maybe that's why phrases like "guilt sometimes catches up with me" or "lucky breaks of travel" seem too stiff; the rest, by comparison, is so fluid. From those who give much we expect much. Don't forget, while you are scoring, to think about whether a piece holds your attention. This one is a favorite of mine. To appreciate it even more, try reading it aloud.

Paper C is pleasant and inoffensive. Its theme is clear and somewhat developed. We have the feeling that the writer could have done more if she had been more interested in her subject. She has chosen something (I suspect) that seems "right" for this assignment, though it is not really what interests her most. Still, she has a certain pride in her spoon collection, and it's a good choice in one respect: Not many other students responding to this prompt would select this particular topic. This means that her paper has a better chance of standing out. Some phrases, such as "charming spoons," seem a little forced, while others, such as "my disastrous room," sound more natural. It's a paper in which voice comes and goes—always a hard call.

The writer needs to let go a little more, which she might have done with another topic. Conventionally, this paper is stronger than it is weak, despite some curious spelling errors: How does it happen that *Europe* and *appreciate* are spelled correctly, while *cupple* and *circul* are not? This paper also suffers, as many papers do, from overparagraphing, which is a symbol, in this instance, of underdevelopment, since paragraphs usually come at the right spots. The paragraphs are skeletal and flimsy, however, which makes the whole piece more tottery, less substantial. Yet, while it moves too quickly from point to point, it does remain focused on the main topic and offers enough detail to convey the writer's ideas.

Sample Papers D, E, and F

Now that we have defined the range of our holistic scoring scale in terms of the three previous anchor papers (which represent the high, middle, and low points on the scale), we are ready to do some practice holistic scoring.

Read the following papers, comparing them to the anchor papers A, B, and C that you just scored, and consider the full list of traits: quality and completeness of ideas, development of ideas, organization, voice, word choice, sentence structure and fluency, and conventions. Remember to assign just *one* score per paper, reflecting (1) how the traits work in balance and (2) how the paper compares in overall quality to the anchor papers. (Remember, Paper A scored 1; Paper B scored 5; and Paper C scored 3.)

Write your score in the blank at the end of each practice paper or on a piece of scratch paper, if you prefer. Remember that you can use *all* the score points on the 5-point scale. So, if you find a paper that is a little better than a 1 (Paper A) but not quite up to a 3 (Paper C), assign it a 2. The same is true of papers that fall between 3 and 5; assign them a score of 4.

Suggested scores will be given at the end of the section, together with comments. All papers are written to the prompt, "Write about a favorite object that is important to you." All are midlevel (junior high school) papers.

PAPER D

I'm writing about the gun cause it is important to me.
Why is it important to me. Cause if we americans didn't have
    guns we would be dangered by many things on earth.
Just how do you think we americans took victory over the british.
If we didn't have guns we wouldn't be able to hunt.
We couldn't target at anything.
We also couldn't use self defense.
I also like guns cause they are loud.
Guns are very expensive.
Guns come in many colors.
Guns mostly are black.
You can find guns in many assortments.
Guns can also be dangerous.
Guns come from new to old.
They can rust too.
You haf't to clean your guns.
You need bulletts for them.
You also need a holster.
Some guns need clips.
And some guns can backfire.
And guns are easy to use.

SCORE (1 to 5) _____

PAPER E

The past is very important to me, theres events and special people I like to remember. Thinking back on the memories I've had is very enjoyable, some are bad and some are good, but I don't like to think about the bad ones. I've had a pretty good past, I've lived in many different places, Chicagos been the best!

and I've also had many neat friends its neat to be at home thinking about a friend that you've had goodtimes with and beable to call them up and get together again for new experiences.

Some people don't like to think about the past, they would rather go on with the future, not me! the past will always important to me because everyday is part of the future and the past. I exspecialy like old movies. they made more musicals with dancing and stuff then they do now, mostly what they make now is horror movies with blood and pain, they're not bad, but there not great either.

SCORE (1 to 5) ――――――

PAPER F

The object that has a lot of meaning to me would be a coat I had way back in the second grade.

The coat was the kind that had a silk outside and a white kind of cotton on the inside. It also had pockets on the inside, and was the kind of coat you could turn inside out and wear.

I used to wear that coat all the time.

It was like part of my life the way a baby has to hold onto its blanket to keep from crying. Well thats the way the coat was to me because everytime I put it on it was like a whole new me. Sounds kind of dumb but that was the way it was. See, whenever I got on the swings to play bomber, or WWI flying ace, I couldn't be those people without my coat.

I had that coat for almost five years of my life. My parents kept on telling me to throw it way becaise It looked funny on me since I had out grown it. But I couldn't do that since I had done so much stuff in the jacket like football, baseball, and going down to the pond to catch salamanders.

I did finally stop wearing my jacket around the summer of 1985. I finally noticed that the sleeves only came down to my elbows. But I still got it in my closet. I don't think I'll ever throw it away. I even try it on sometimes although it doesn't fit. So I would say that jacket is a meaningful object to me.

SCORE (1 to 5) ――――――

Suggested Scores and Comments (Papers D, E, and F)

The suggested scores in this section are just that—suggestions. Even trained, experienced raters who have been scoring for many years see different things in papers. Therefore, if your scores are within a point of the suggested scores (either way), it may simply be that you see something in the paper that other raters have not noticed or that you are placing more emphasis on one aspect of the paper than another (e.g., attending more to conventions than to voice). If, however, your scores differ from the suggested scores by two points or more, we recommend that you reread the paper and rethink your scores carefully. What is most important, however, is not so much the score itself but the thinking process by which you arrived at your score. You should feel comfortable *describing what you see in each paper that causes you to score it as you do.*

PAPER D: 1-2

The conventions and sentence structure are the strongest traits within this paper, despite problems with capitalization and a total absence of respect for the paragraph. The serious problems in this paper, however, are a constant shift in focus and a lack of development. The paper is merely a list of statements that take the reader to no particular conclusion. Further, the obvious nature of the statements (e.g., "they are loud," "You need bulletts for them") takes them out of the realm of observation; they are just space fillers. This student doesn't seem to care what he is writing, and as a result, we lose interest, too.

PAPER E: 1-2

On the face of it, this paper seems a bit better written than paper D, but, in fact, it says almost nothing. It's awash in generalities, drifting aimlessly. It has a floaty, untextured tone. The comment on movies at the end is as close as the paper comes to specificity, which isn't very close. Further, it waffles. The movies aren't bad, but they're not great either. What exactly does this writer think? We don't find out. This isn't a paper in which either writer or reader learns much.

PAPER F: 4

This writer seems to enjoy himself, to have a good time with the topic, and to write easily. The voice is strong; the word choice is natural. It's a bit of a sleeper—deceptively simple but very appealing.

Read it aloud, and you'll see that some spots flow very well, while others bump along a bit. The conventions aren't bad. There are minor problems but none that polishing would not take care of. Stronger verbs would give this piece some of the punch that it now lacks, but the imagery is surprisingly effective despite the quiet tone. Did you give this paper a 3? If so, you're not alone in your response, but I think it has more voice than that. Read it once more to see whether you agree.

Note: Suggested analytical scores for these three papers are included at the end of the next section, on pages 57–58.

ANALYTICAL ASSESSMENT

In this part of the chapter, you'll be scoring papers analytically, using the scoring guide described on the following few pages. Remember that now your task is to assign scores by measuring each performance against the written criteria in the scoring guide. This guide is presented on pages 29 through 36, and you can refer to it there. You may wish to photocopy it so that you can keep it flat on the table beside you as you are scoring. It is six pages long (one page per trait).

This time you will not use anchor papers to assist you in assigning scores. Even though we usually do provide them in analytical training, space limitations won't permit us to provide enough papers to give you a thorough set of references for each score on each of the six traits. Anchor papers are helpful, though, and if you decide to use this system to train colleagues or to teach your students to score papers, you can assemble your own set of anchor papers from those you score as a group.

Not all of the following papers will be written to the same prompt, but we don't think that you'll find the shifts too difficult. After all, if you let students select their own topics (as we suggest in the next chapter), you'll be seeing some variety anyway.

The more papers you score, the easier the process will become, so we encourage you to extend your practice by using your own or another teacher's student papers. Practice with a colleague if possible, so that you can compare and discuss results. This is how you will train yourself to score well.

How to Score

Each paper that you score will receive six separate scores, one for each trait. The total scoring guide includes the following six traits:

Ideas and content
Organization
Voice
Word choice
Sentence fluency
Conventions

You should take care in scoring to keep the traits as distinct as possible and not to let your impression of, say, conventions, influence your impression of, say, ideas. Some papers may have very consistent scores across all six traits, while other papers will have very different scores on different traits.

Notice that the scoring guide presents definitions (criteria) for the various traits at the 5, 3, and 1 score levels. Levels 4 and 2 are not defined in writing (in order to keep the scoring guide from becoming so long that no one would read it), but you should assign the full range of scores—5, 4, 3, 2, *and* 1—as appropriate.

Think of a score of 3 as representing a balance between strong and weak with respect to a particular trait. At the 4 level, strengths begin to outweigh weaknesses, and at the 5 level, strengths are dominant. Similarly, at the 2 level, weaknesses begin to outweigh strengths, while at the 1 level, few if any strengths are evident with respect to the trait being scored (though, remember, there may be strengths in other traits).

Keep in mind, too, that scores are not discrete points in space. Rather, they exist along a continuum, as shown in Figure 2.1. In other words, there is a *range* of 5s, a *range* of 4s, a *range* of 3s, and so on. Some 5s are a bit stronger than others. Further, the criteria, specific and well defined though they may be, may not fit a given paper perfectly. Each student's effort is unique. These criteria are an attempt to capture the *essence* of what you're likely to see in the writing of many students; and our experience scoring thousands of papers using this guide suggests that, in fact, the descriptions are very accurate. Nevertheless, some papers will not match precisely what is written in the guide. Make the best guess that you can about the score in such a case, keeping in mind that what matters most in assigning scores is judging the extent to which strengths and weaknesses balance or the extent to which one outweighs the other.

Notice in Figure 2.1 that a strong 3 (or 3+) is actually *closer* along the continuum to a weak 4 (or 4−) than it is to a weak 3 (or 3-). This visualization is the basis for the argument that in assessment a 1-point difference may still be regarded as agreement. In fact, raters often think to themselves, "Yes, it's a 3, but it's a high 3, almost a 4," or "It's a 4 but just barely—really more 3-ish." Thus, we discover that as raters verbalize the reasons behind their scores, apparent mathematical differences are often philosophically very small. In addition, however, there is the notion that multiple reactions simply enrich, and in some ways strengthen, the overall response to the paper. We'll say more about this in the context of classroom assessment, which is generally more tolerant of such differences. For now, let's simply state that given enlightened and defensible subjectivity, in which scores are tied to agreed-upon criteria, a 1-point difference in scores between any two raters should not make anyone uncomfortable.

While they are scoring, some raters find it helpful to think of the total message that scores taken together provide the writer. What message does the rater want to give? Perhaps the voice is powerful, while the sentence structure is the weak spot in the paper. Let your scores

One of the most trustworthy evaluations we can produce is a "mixed bag": an evaluation made up of the verdicts or perceptions of two or more observers who *may not agree* (Elbow, 1987, 223).

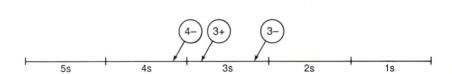

FIGURE 2.1. Scoring Continuum

represent this message as well as you can. Also, remember that at the classroom level, analytical scores represent feedback, not final judgments.

The scoring guide is followed by sample papers for you to score. You are asked to score the first group of papers on only two traits: ideas and content, and organization. Then you are asked to score the next group of papers on four traits: ideas and content, organization, voice, and word choice. Finally, you'll score the last group of papers on all six traits: ideas and content, organization, voice, word choice, sentence fluency, and conventions. This approach lets you ease into the task of scoring without having to keep all six traits in your head the first time around.

Later, if you want to go back and score the earlier papers for all six traits, you may do so. We provide suggested scores for only the traits we ask you to rate, but you can compare your scores with those of a colleague or students in your class. Space is provided for you to write your scores within the text, but you may prefer to write them on scratch paper.

By the way, we strongly recommend that you (1) study the scoring guide, (2) photocopy it for handy reference, (3) score all twelve practice papers, and (4) read our suggested scores and commentary all at one sitting. We estimate that this will take about an hour, or a little more if you read and discuss papers with a colleague as you go (which is an excellent way of getting the most out of this exercise). Plan to set aside some undisturbed time for this task; it will make the discussions that follow more useful to you.

ANALYTICAL SCORING GUIDE *

The Six Traits

IDEAS AND CONTENT

Score of 5. This paper is clear, focused, and interesting. It holds the reader's attention. Relevant anecdotes and details enrich the central theme or story line.

---

*The original scoring guide on which this one is based was developed in 1984 by a group of seventeen teachers from the Beaverton (Oregon) School District #48, working in conjunction with Vicki Spandel, who has been a writing consultant to the district since 1984. Since the original guide appeared, it has undergone numerous revisions and refinements, based on suggestions from teachers throughout the Northwest who have used it in classrooms with their own students or who have used it to score student writing at district and state levels. The original guide now exists in multiple versions, most of which comprise the six traits from the original version. Teachers in various districts use their own variations of the guide when they are teaching writing and scoring papers. The version printed in this book is a revised copy of an early (1984) draft.

The writer seems to be writing from experience and shows insight: a good sense of how events unfold, how people respond to life and to each other, and how ideas relate.

Supporting, relevant, telling details give the reader important information that he or she could not personally bring to the text. This writer seems to notice what others might overlook.

The writing has balance: Main ideas stand out; secondary ideas do not usurp too much attention.

The writer seems in control and orchestrates development of the topic in an enlightening, entertaining way.

The writer works with and shapes ideas, making connections and sharing insights that reflect his or her own thinking.

3. The paper is clear and focused, even though the overall result may not be especially captivating. Support is attempted, but it may be limited or obvious, insubstantial, too general, or out of balance with the main ideas.

The writer may or may not be writing from experience but, either way, has difficulty going from general observations to specific points or useful insights.

The writer seems to have considered ideas but only superficially and in a way that enables the reader readily to second-guess the plot or the main points of the text.

Ideas, though reasonably clear, often tend toward the mundane; the reader is not sorry to see the paper end.

Conclusions or main points seem to echo observations heard elsewhere; only on occasion do they seem to reflect the writer's own thinking.

Supporting details tend to be skimpy, general, or predictable.

Control is sporadic; the writer is beginning to define the topic but isn't there yet.

1. The paper lacks a central idea or purpose, or forces the reader to make inferences based on very sketchy details.

Information is very limited or simply unclear.

Details do not ring true; they evolve from clichés, platitudes, or stereotypes and not from the writer's own thinking or experience.

Attempts at development may be minimal or may clutter up the text with random thoughts from which no central theme emerges.

The writer has not begun to define the topic in any meaningful or personal way.

ORGANIZATION

5. The organization enhances and showcases the central idea or theme. The order, structure, or presentation is compelling and moves the reader through the text.

Details seem to fit where they're placed.

An inviting introduction draws the reader in, and a satisfying conclusion leaves the reader with a sense of resolution.

Transitions are smooth and weave the separate threads of meaning into one cohesive whole.

Organization flows so smoothly that the reader may not be conscious of organizational patterns or structures unless looking for them.

3. The reader can readily follow what's being said, but the overall organization may sometimes be ineffective or too obvious.

The introduction and conclusion are recognizable, though not so well crafted or well connected to the central theme as the reader might wish.

Placement or relevance of some details leaves the reader occasionally confused or impatient.

The paper sometimes moves along at a good pace but at other times bogs down in trivia or speeds along too rapidly.

Transitions sometimes work well; at other times, the connections between ideas seem forced, inappropriate, or too easily anticipated.

Despite problems, the organization does not seriously get in the way of the main point or the story line.

1. Organization is haphazard and disjointed. The writing lacks direction, with ideas, details, or events strung together helter-skelter.

There is no clearly identifiable introduction or conclusion.

Transitions are very weak, leaving connections between ideas fuzzy, incomplete, or bewildering.

Details often serve only to confuse the reader or to fill space; they do not contribute to the central theme or the purpose of the text.

Noticeable gaps in information confuse and confound the reader.

Pacing is consistently awkward, so that the reader feels either mired down in irrelevant trivia or rushed along at a breathless pace.

Lack of organization ultimately obscures or distorts the main point or the purpose of the text.

VOICE

5. The writer speaks directly to the reader in a way that is individualistic, expressive, and engaging. Clearly, the writer is involved in the text and is writing to be read.

The paper is honest and written from the heart. It has the ring of conviction.

The language is natural yet provocative; it brings the topic to life.

The reader feels a strong sense of interaction with the writer and senses the person behind the words.

The projected tone and voice clarify and give flavor to the writer's message.

3. The writer seems sincere but not fully involved in the topic. The result is pleasant, acceptable, sometimes even personable, but not compelling.

The writer seems to weigh words carefully, to keep a safe distance between writer and reader, to avoid risk, and to write what he or she thinks the reader wants.

The writing tends to hide rather than reveal the writer.

The writing communicates in an earnest but fairly routine manner, and only occasionally amuses, surprises, delights, or moves the reader.

Voice may emerge strongly on occasion, only to shift or to disappear a line or two later behind a facade of general, vague, or abstract language.

1. The writer seems wholly indifferent, uninvolved, or dispassionate. As a result, the writing is flat, lifeless, stiff, or mechanical. It may be (depending on the topic) overly technical or jargonistic.

The reader has no sense of the writer behind the words and no sense of a real desire on the part of the writer to communicate.

The writer seems to speak in a kind of monotone that flattens all potential highs or lows of the message.

The writing communicates on a functional level, at best, without moving or involving the reader at all.

Delivery is so consistently flat that the reader may find it hard to focus on the message even when the wording seems reasonably clear and correct.

WORD CHOICE

5. Words convey the intended message in an interesting, precise, and natural way. The writing is full and rich, yet concise.

Words are specific and accurate; they seem just right.

Imagery is strong.

Powerful verbs give the writing energy.

Vocabulary may be striking, but it's natural, and never overdone.

Expression is fresh and appealing; slang is used sparingly.

3. The language is quite ordinary, but it does convey the message: It's functional, even if it lacks punch. Often, the writer settles for what's easy or handy, producing a sort of "generic paper" stuffed with familiar words and phrases.

The language communicates but rarely captures the reader's imagination. While the overall meaning is quite clear, some words may lack precision.

The writer rarely experiments with language; however, the paper *may* have some fine moments.

Attempts at colorful or poetic language often seem overdone and calculated to impress the reader.

Images lack detail and often depend on the reader's own knowledge of the topic.

Clichés, redundancies, and hackneyed phrases are common.

A few key verbs may liven things up, but equally often, abstract, general, or flat language robs the text of power.

1. The writer struggles with a limited vocabulary, groping for words to convey meaning. Often the language is so vague and abstract or so redundant and devoid of detail that only the broadest, most general sort of message comes through.

Words are consistently dull, colorless, or abstract. There is little for the reader to grasp.

Monotonous repetition or overwhelming reliance on worn, threadbare expressions repeatedly clouds or smothers the message.

Often words simply do not fit the text: They seem imprecise, inadequate, or just plain wrong.

Imagery is very fuzzy or absent altogether; the text is "peopled" only with generalities.

Verbs are weak and few in number; *is, are, was, were* dominate.

SENTENCE FLUENCY

5. The writing has an easy flow and rhythm when read aloud. Sentences are well built, with consistently strong and varied structure that makes expressive oral reading easy and enjoyable.

Sentence structure reflects logic and sense, helping to show how ideas relate.

The writing sounds natural and fluent; it glides along with effective phrasing, one sentence flowing effortlessly into the next.

Writing is appropriately concise, yet not terse. Sentences display an effective combination of power and grace.

Sentences vary in structure and length, adding interest to the text.

Fragments, if used at all, work well.

Dialogue, if used, sounds natural.

3. Sentences tend to be mechanical rather than fluid. The text hums along efficiently for the most part, though it may lack a certain rhythm or grace, tending to be more pleasant than musical. Occasional awkward constructions force the reader to slow down or reread.

Sentence structure sometimes clearly conveys relationships between ideas, and sometimes not. Connections between phrases or sentences may be less fluid than desired.

The writer shows good control with simple sentence structure but variable control over complex syntax.

Sentences sometimes vary in length or structure, but, for the most part, the writer falls into a pattern and sticks with it.

Fragments, if used, sometimes work but sometimes seem the result of oversight.

Dialogue, if used, sometimes rings true but sometimes sounds forced or contrived.

Sentences, though functional, often lack energy.

Some parts of the text invite expressive oral reading; others may be a bit stiff.

1. The paper is difficult to follow or to read aloud. Sentences tend to be choppy, incomplete, rambling, irregular, or just very awkward.

Nonstandard English syntax is common. Word patterns are often jarring and irregular, and far removed from the way people usually write or speak.

Sentence structure does not generally enhance meaning. In fact, it may obscure meaning.

Most sentences seem disjointed, awkward, confused, or nonsensical. They may begin one way and then go off in another direction altogether.

Word patterns often subject the reader to relentlessly monotonous rhythms (e.g., subject-verb or subject-verb-object).

The text does not invite—and may not even permit—expressive oral reading.

CONVENTIONS

5. The writer demonstrates a good grasp of standard writing conventions (e.g., grammar, capitalization, punctuation, usage, spelling, paragraphing) and uses them effectively to enhance readability. Errors tend to be so few and so minor that the reader can easily skim right over them unless specifically searching for them.

Paragraphing tends to be sound and to reinforce the organizational structure.

Grammar and usage are correct and contribute to clarity and style.

Punctuation is smooth and guides the reader through the text.

Spelling is generally correct, even on more difficult words.

The writer may manipulate conventions—particularly grammar—for stylistic effect.

The writing is sufficiently long and complex to allow the writer to show skill in using a wide range of conventions.

Only light editing would be required to polish the text for publication.

3. Errors in writing conventions, while not overwhelming, begin to impair readability. While errors do not block meaning, they tend to be distracting.

Paragraphing may be inconsistent. Paragraphs sometimes run together or begin in the wrong places.

Terminal (end-of-sentence) punctuation is almost always correct; internal punctuation, however, may be incorrect or missing altogether.

Spelling is usually correct, or reasonably phonetic, on common words.

Problems with usage are not severe enough to distort meaning.

The writer may show reasonable control over a very limited range of conventions, but the text may be too simple or too short to reflect real mastery of conventions.

Errors in all areas tend to show some consistency, for example, a writer may misspell a word the same way throughout the text.

Moderate (more than light but less than extensive) editing would be required to polish the text for publication.

Some errors are minor and seem to reflect hasty editing.

1. Numerous errors in usage, sentence structure, spelling, or punctuation repeatedly distract the reader and make the text difficult to read. In fact, the severity and the frequency of errors tend to be so overwhelming that the reader finds it very difficult to focus on the message and must reread for meaning.

The writer shows very limited skill in using conventions.

Basic punctuation (including terminal punctuation) tends to be omitted, haphazard, or incorrect.

Spelling errors are frequent, even on common words, and are not always phonetic.

Paragraphing may be highly irregular, absent altogether, or so frequent (every sentence) that it bears no relation to the organizational structure of the text.

Extensive (e.g., more than moderate) editing would be required to polish the text for publication.

SAMPLE PAPERS 1-3: ANALYTICAL SCORING OF TWO TRAITS

Ideas and Content, and Organization

Score the following papers for *two traits:* ideas and content, and organization. Remember that each paper will receive *two* scores, one for each trait.

1. MAKING DECISIONS

Making decisions requires a lot of thinking and evaluating. First of all, when making a decision you must take time and not rush into your conclusion. Clarify what you are deciding about, making sure you understand it thoroughly, without any confusion. Reason out what your concluding decision will effect. Ask yourself who is involved, or will be involved, and whether or not they may be effected also. Question whether or not these effects will be positive or negative. Hopefully, they turn out to be positive.

Furthermore, devise ahead of time other alternatives, if there are any that may be taken, and again decide who and what may be effected. Another option in decision making may be to ask other people their opinion on the subject. Be aware that their opinion may not be correct, and you do not have to follow what they think or feel. The information given to you by others is only an opinion; their opinion. Eventually, your decision will have impact on other things. Until you have constituted your decision, you will be unaware of the results. Just be sure to take your time to think about everything that's effected, and be careful in the end.

SCORES (1-5)

Ideas and content: _____

Organization: _____

2. ON THE TRAIL

There is something special about being outside running dogs on a cool, crisp day. You are out in the middle of the woods, the snow is glistening off the trees and the ground. The birds are almost always singing in the trees. They stop singing suddenly and fly away as you come racing closer, then it's dead silent.

If you listen closely you can hear the runners whispering across the snow and hear the pitter-patter of the dogs' feet hitting the hard packed trail and see the breath from the dogs curl around their faces like wreaths, covering their faces with a clear white frost. You come up on two trails, one going to the right and the other to the left. As you get closer, you can see the leaders' ears go back and forth, waiting intensely for a signal as you move to the fork in the trail.

Then 'Bam' you break the dead silence by yelling 'Haw' to your leaders, to go left. They go left, then the silence sets back in on you. Up ahead there's a corner, you set yourself, your ready, here goes, swish around goes your team. The front of the sled, then the whole sled goes sliding sideways. You use skill and muscle to keep the sled from tipping over. After your around the corner, you straighten the sled back up. Your going thru a brushy part of the trail. You know that there are moose out in the brush.

When you reach the brushy area your heart starts beating, you constantly watch your dogs for signs of 'moose ahead'. You also watch the trail behind you for figures of moose standing there.

Two minutes have passed and you thought it was a half hour of craning your neck and staring off into the brush with your heart beating while going thru the brushy part of the trail. You breathe a sigh of relief for not having any trouble with moose.

By now your almost home, nothing but a long, steep hill ahead, then home. You reach the base of the hill, you encourage your dogs to keep running. You run behind the sled, whistling and pushing the sled, helping them along. You finally reach the top. You are exhausted from the run up the long, steep hill.

You jump back onto the runner and give a couple of kicks and away you go.

A minute later your in your dog lot. You give each dog a big hug and pet them and tell them what good dogs they are while you are unhooking them and chaining them up. After you finish hooking them up you brush off the breath crystals that have formed on their faces.

After the dogs, sled and harness are all put away you give each dog a dish of warm broth plus their dog food. Cherish this day and time on the trail for tomorrow may hold a lot of depressing times for you.

SCORES (1-5)

Ideas and content: _____

Organization: _____

3. MY WATCH AND MY STEREO

The thing I like the most is my sterio its realy cool. I got it for Christmas. I was so supprised that I got it. I never got a radio for Christmas before. I got a wtch to for Christmas. I like my watch it has buttons and stuff on it. I like my sterio the best though.

Because its the most expensive thing I got for Christmas. My sisters got me the sterio and my dad got me the watch. I think I like the most is my sterio and my watch. I like my sterio the most because it is loud and I just about break the windows of our house I like my watch because it beeps every hour and it bugs the teachers to death. I like my radio and watch both. My watch that I got is digital. My radio goes realy loud it has 4 speakers. Its AM, FM sterio dual cassete player. It has an amplifier right by the speakers.

Everyone likes my sterio because its dual cassete and its realy neat. Everyone likes my watch to because it has buttons on the top of it.

SCORES (1-5)

Ideas and content: _____

Organization: _____

Now let's look at the next two traits: *voice* and *word choice*.

A Word About Scoring Voice

In scoring workshops, voice is the trait that inevitably commands the most attention. It's arguably the most interesting trait, but also—to many people—the most mysterious. "What is it?" they ask.

Here's a way of looking at voice that may help. Suppose you were given the following bit of text:

. . . and so there ain't nothing more to write about, and I am rotten glad of it, because if I'd 'a' knowed what a trouble it was to make a book I wouldn't 'a' tackled it, and ain't a-going to no more.

And were asked who wrote the passage:

1. Edgar Allan Poe
2. Mark Twain
3. Richard Nixon

The trait that tells you the writer is Mark Twain is *voice*. (This passage is from *Huckleberry Finn*.)

The writings of Donald Graves and Donald Murray, which are themselves alive with voice, abound with good descriptions of what voice is and why we as writing teachers should care about it. But no one has written more eloquently on voice than Peter Elbow:

> *Writing with no voice is dead, mechanical, faceless. It lacks any sound. Writing with no voice may be saying something true, important, or new; it may be logically organized; it may even be a work of genius. But it is as though the words came through some kind of mixer rather than being uttered by a person. Extreme lack of voice is characteristic of bureaucratic memos, technical engineering writing, much sociology, many textbooks:*
>
> > *Tests should reflect changes in learned behavior; the normal utilization of reliability estimates must be revised since it is assumed that we are not measuring a trait or innate mental capacity but rather an acquired skill or concept which can be measured incrementally. Thus scores should reflect changes from one administration to the next. [From an essay on adult education.]*
>
> *Nobody is at home here. In its extreme form, no voice is the army-manual style (Elbow, 1981, 287-288).*

The writing process has a driving force called voice. . . . To ignore voice is to present the process as a lifeless, mechanical act. Divorcing voice from process is like omitting salt from stew, love from sex, or sun from gardening (Graves, 1983, 227).

Each of us, as we read and write, develops an ear for voice. We may hear other voices first, but come in time, as every writer must, to hear our own. Various teachers, as they work to score the trait of voice, have defined it in the following ways:

1. "A clear indication of the personality or 'personal stamp' of the writer."
2. "It's involvement, experience that can be communicated, a connection, caring, phrasing."
3. "Strong self-expression, involvement, belief in what one writes."
4. "Expressing yourself."
5. "Sharing your feelings, openness, taking risks, showing that you care for your subject."
6. "Uniqueness of ideas and phrasing that reflects the writer's personality and ideas."

Voice separates writing that is read from writing that is not read (Murray, 1985, 73).

7. "Expressing one's thoughts and feelings on paper."

8. "Personal feelings that a reader can sense while reading someone's writing."

9. "Honestly and truthfully telling about your experiences."

10. "The genuineness of the material written as conceived by the writer."

11. "It's what I am inside—what I'm wishing I will be (anticipation)—what I'm wishing I was (pretending)."

12. "The ability to convey personal emotion and experience."

13. "Realistic presentation of the writer that elicits a feeling or emotion in the reader."

14. "Speaking honestly from experience—letting people know who you are—how you feel—being willing to express yourself freely."

15. "The feeling that you are part of the story—'Hey, this could be me,' or 'I wish this was me'—I'm not only reading, I'm living this story.'"

16. "The person is revealed in the writing."

17. "Mood, feeling, tone (ability to tell the truth)."

18. "The inner self expressing and sharing the writer's ideas in the writing."

19. "Voice comes from within the person—the real you, so to speak. Voice is your feelings, your thoughts. Voice is something of value or importance to you."

20. "Willingness to share a bit of one's personality."

21. "Revealing your vulnerabilities—but, there needs to be enough knowledge about the subject to let your own voice show through."

22. "A window through which we look, to see what the writer is all about."

23. "The ability—and the courage—to tell the truth."

24. "A hearty combination of conscience and soul."

As you have seen, I am a writer who came of a sheltered life. A sheltered life can be a daring life as well. For all serious daring starts from within (Welty, 1983, 114).

Within, amid, and between these various definitions you may find your own.

A Word About Scoring Word Choice

The nuclear industry has a phrase for things that go wrong all the time: "normally occurring abnormal occurrences." The world of euphemistic jargon is the world in which "second-hand" cars become "experienced," a hospital death is "a therapeutic misadventure," and an airline reports a fatal aircrash to its stockholders as "the involuntary conversion of a 727" (McCrum, Cran, and McNeil, 1986, 345).

Beware of the writer who is trying to bedazzle you with the weekly vocabulary list. A good vocabulary flows from the writer's reading and experience. It isn't something that the writer reaches for out of need like an umbrella on a hook. The message must come first. Often the power in a successful piece comes less from esoteric or unusual words than from the writer's skill in using everyday words well.

SAMPLE PAPERS 4-7: ANALYTICAL SCORING OF FOUR TRAITS

Ideas and Content, Organization, Voice, and Word Choice

Score the following papers for *four traits:* ideas and content, organization, voice, and word choice. Each paper will receive *four* scores, one for each trait.

4. DARKNESS ENGULFS ME

Darkness engulfes me. Rain pelts down upon me. Crushing, it seems, as it hits my aching body. It is comong down fast, falling in sheets. I try to look ahead, But I can see no thing.

I have been traveling on foot for days. My clothes are tatters, Mud and grime cover them. My shoes have wholes in the soles, allowing water to wash my unsocked feet.

My stomach growls in anguish. I haven't eaten but berries for a long while.

I think I am on a road. Every so often a car will pass. I haven't come upon a house. If I can only go on until I do.

I don't know how I got here. All I do know is that I want to find a house.

I keep falling. I want to lay and rest, But if I lie still I get very chilled. I feel as though I can't go on.

I can't take anymore. As I collapse the rain suddenly halts. In the distance I notice a single light. A house light!

That house means everything to me. It reminds me of happiness, home, warmth, and friendship.

It gives me a new hope I get up and begin to run.

SCORES (1-5)

Ideas and content: _____

Organization: _____

Voice: _____

Word choice: _____

5. SPECIAL FRIEND

"A special friend, huh? Gimme a break! What do you mean, 'special friend'?" That's what I thought when I first received this topic. "Oh brother," is more like it. Then I began to take the subject seriously. I have quite a few friends, but when the chips are down, who can take the heat?

I have four real friends that I spent alot of time with. Jack? Is he the one I can rely on? No, we have alot in common, and we help each other often, but when it comes to the end of the rope, it's every man for himself. I could probably rely upon Chad, but that's how it is when a friendship is new. We aren't really that close. The only other friends I have are Bob and Tom. Tom is a great friend, but quite often we are fighting over one thing or another. I wouldn't want to be stuck behind enemy lines with him for long.

That leaves Bob. So, is he my "special friend" (ugh, I hate that phrase)? Is he my kemosabe? Well, what is it that might make him so?

He and I share alot of the same interests. Science Fiction or Fantasy Adventure style stories are our favorites (from Raiders of the Lost Ark to Star Wars). We both like the same music and games. The two of us spend our time drawing the same things. You could always find us riding bikes to and from school. Oh, and by the way, we both collect comic books.

By the way?! Am I nuts?!? Comic book collecting is our way of life. Every Wednesday, we go down to the House of Fantasy to pick up our reserved copies. We each collect 21 titles, only six of which we don't have in common. We read them together, and then we file them away together. We jointly predict the outcomes of the stories and try to pick up on the deeper aspects of the magazines.

One reason we are such good friends is that we live very close to each other. It is simply a hop, skip, and a jump to his house. A hop off my street to Park, a skip down Park to Crestview, and a jump down the hill to his house. Is it fate, or just coincidence?!?

As I mentioned, we both collect comics. We have now become business partners in a soon-to-become deal with Dell Comics. We hope to become writers for them and we are working hard toward this goal.

So, is Bob my best friend? I think so. We will hopefully stay friends despite career hassles, and should grow old and wise together. As Sun Tzu once said, "Join your forces and you shall become invincible."

SCORES (1–5)

> **Ideas and content:** _____
>
> **Organization:** _____
>
> **Voice:** _____
>
> **Word choice:** _____

6. SHOES

People are important to me. The weather is important to me. But objects are not that important to me. No one I am close to has died on me. No one has left me anything to remember them by. No one has given me anything truly special. I am young. And these are things I have not yet experienced. So honestly, the only object I can think of that is of any importants to me is my shoes. That's right my shoes. Besides the fact that I think shoes are important to a person's charictor I am really glad to have them. I have what you call tender feet. You don't see me walking around without my shoes in the grass, on the beach, or anywhere else. It literally kills my feet. It hurts. I hate it. And there is no other way to put it. So you see I may not have a special rock given to me by my grandfather who has passed away or I may not have a gold band to match the one of my lover's. But I am proud to say that I have shoes. Yes good old shoes. And thats good enough for me.

SCORES (1-5)

Ideas and content: _____

Organization: _____

Voice: _____

Word choice: _____

7. FISH TANK

I found the fish tank in the pantry filled with 20 year-old bottles of pickles. My sister and I had only the pantry left. We had already made countless trips to the landfill, saved many items, and given some away. The minute I saw the tank, I knew immediately that I had to have it.

I couldn't wait to fill it and dump a few fish in. Little to my knowledge were there so [many] commitments involved!

I had the water curing on the deck in the bank for a week. I had made several trips to the fish store. Never had I noticed so many things I could buy! My mind soon outgrew my pocketbook. I had decisions to make about money-matters.

I had reached a peak in the assessory imagination. I had all things necessary to get a start.

After a while, my tank transformed into an energy release. A weekend getaway type of thing. I have spent countless hours just on general maintenance!

Yes, at times I have wanted to just throw it out the window. For the time being, it's tolerable. In fact, I can barely imagine my room without it! The constant buzzing of the pumps rocks me to sleep at night.

SCORES (1-5)

Ideas and content: _____

Organization: _____

Voice: _____

Word choice: _____

A Word About Scoring Sentence Fluency

Writing is to some extent an aural skill. Some readers hear the writing in their heads as they read. Others hear only silence. Therefore, it's a good idea, while you are learning to score sentence structure, to read papers aloud and also to hear them read aloud by others. (It's also an excellent idea for students in the classroom to hear papers, lots of them, and to read aloud to each other.)

When you are analyzing papers for sentence fluency, do not think about punctuation too much. Think about how the sentences would sound if they were punctuated correctly. Truly faulty sentence structure rarely can be fixed by shuffling commas and periods around. (Not that faulty punctuation isn't a problem; it just isn't the same kind of problem.) Sentence fluency deals primarily with sentence flow and with rhythm. As you score, also keep in mind that sentence fragments are fine if they work. Don't ask yourself whether the writer intended them. It doesn't matter. If they work, the chances are that they're intentional or, at the very least, that the writer has a good ear. Better still.

Activities which place children in the role of observers are those which establish the attitudes that language is constantly changing and that usage items mastered today may not be the most acceptable ones when they are adults (Pooley, 1974, 75).

A Word About Scoring Conventions

Conventions are scored as a function of readability, meaning that in a strong paper, conventions are so well handled that they make the task of reading simple. Appropriate capitalization, well-placed punctuation, correct spelling, and proper grammar and usage make reading—silently or aloud—easier. There are no alarmingly wrong notes.

Papers at the 5 level need not be flawless. Errors tend to be minor and almost unnoticeable. They don't jump out at you and do not offend your editorial sense of what's right or appropriate.

While you are scoring, it may help you to ask yourself how much work would be required to edit and polish the text. At the 5 level, the answer is very little—almost none. At the 3 level, moderate work would be required, and at the 1 level, extensive work would be required, assuming that all major revision of ideas and organization were complete.

SAMPLE PAPERS 8-12: ANALYTICAL SCORING OF SIX TRAITS

Ideas and Content, Organization, Voice, Word Choice, Sentence Fluency, and Conventions

Score the following papers for *all six traits:* ideas and content, organization, voice, word choice, sentence fluency, and conventions. Each paper will receive *six* scores, one for each trait.

8. RUNAWAY RALPH

The object that means the most to me is a book called Runaway Ralph. I picked this object because it's a very neat book and I read it a lot. I also really liked it.

I think it's a really neat book because I think it's a whole lot of fun to read. It has a real nice and colorful cover that really appeals to me. Runaway Ralph is all about a little mouse and his motorcycle that runaway together. Since this book has a mouse in it and I really like mice, especially little white ones, I thought it was a really great book. The book was also good because of the number of pages. it wasn't to long and it wasn't to short of a book.

I read this really great book a lot because it's not only exciting but interesting. Runaway Ralph was the first book that I ever read, liked, and not only exciting but interesting too. This book is all the things listed above and more, like fun to read. I thought with all the excitement and interesting parts in the book that it was fun to read. It was also a very good book. With all that stuff going on it's hard to say that it's a bad book. Therefore, in general it's a very good book. I also read it alot because I got it for my 8th birthday.

I really liked it too. It's the best book I have ever read. The book was not too hard to read yet it wasn't too easy to read either. Reading this book really improves my reading skills.

In conclusion I think this publication is a very good learning book. It's also a very fun book to read.

SCORES (1-5)

Ideas and Content: _____   Word choice: _____

Organization: _____   Sentence fluency: _____

Voice: _____   Conventions: _____

9. WINDOW

The Window I Broke

Every time I see the bill for the window I broke, it reminds me of the great time I had at Sun Valley during summer vacation. It also reminds me of the friends I met there, and the places I went while in Sun Valley.

Going to Sun Valley with my friends, Dean and Chad, was the highlight of my summer vacation. It was great because we were staying in our own condo, and we never saw our parents.

It was the best vacation I've ever had. The only bad part was when I accedently broke our window trying to hit a golf ball. The best part was at night in the mall. That's where we found out where all the parties were.

The people I met there made the trip so good. We made about 50 friends in all. Most of the people we met were at the mall, parties, and at Reggie's, a teenage dance club. It's fun when you know almost every person there!

The bill also reminds me of all the different places we went in Sun Valley. One of the best was Reggie's, where we went almost every night. Besides Reggie's, we went to a lot of parties at really nice houses. The swimming pool and the mall were our other major hangouts. We went to alot of weird places while we were there.

Memories of summer vacation, our comrades at Sun Valley, and the different buildings we visited while there, all come back to me when I see the bill for the broken window.

SCORES (1-5)

Ideas and content: _____   Word choice: _____

Organization: _____   Sentence fluency: _____

Voice: _____   Conventions: _____

10. WHAT SCARES ME

What scares me is terrorists. They are (deadly) they can plant bombs, or use rifles or pistols. They can sabotage things, such as planes, cars, boats, and buildings. They could kill you wih a knife (stabing), a pistol or rifle (shooting).

Also you could die anywhere or anyplace.

Terrorists are sneaky. They could be exchange students, also they can be anybody. They disguise themselves, they use camoflage and they could travel with you.

Why are they around. They can be hired by communists. They can show anybody what they can do (terror). Their tired of being themselves. And they probably want to rule the world being terrorists.

Why are there terrorists, They are terrorists for the money for other groups, getting mad at something, they might be foreign criminals, their sick, such as mental health, dope, pills, drunk, and sick in the body. They want attention, to show their leaders, and to show how tough they are.

Where are they from, they are from foreign countries, anywhere around you. There from the Middle East, such as Libya where Khadfy lives somewhere, then they live in Iran, Iraq, and around in the Arab world.

What can America do about it. We can use spies to detect them, When we have them, then we will try them in the Supreme Courts, or in the UN courts. Also we can use spotters to detect them, have heavenly guarded cars with military items inside it, also airlines with bomb detectors, and having the airline with armentent. We can also use security guards and also carry guns.

Therefore what I am scared of hopefully will end with the items I said. Someday I hope (Terrorism) and (Moammor Khadfy) will end someday.

SCORES (1-5)

Ideas and content: _____   Word choice: _____

Organization: _____   Sentence fluency: _____

Voice: _____   Conventions: _____

11. SURVIVAL RIFLE

An object that is special to me is my little .22 calibre survival rifle. I remember the carefree feeling alone in the woods with my dog.

I remember the proud feeling I had when I held up my first rabbit. I remember when my mother used to take me out to look for all kinds of small game.

I remember the closeness that I felt for my mother and father. I remember all of my cousins who used to cram into a little VW rabbit to go look for tomorrow's dinner.

I remember the safe feeling of being warm inside our small, cozy house eating my fresh rabbit that my mother cooked up while outside it was cold and windy. I remember the proud feeling when I presented my quarry to my grandmother, the look on her face and the hug that immediately followed. I remember the contentness I felt to be alone, on my own in the great wilderness, no need to hurry. I remember awakening early in the morning with my father to go hunt moose. I remember the cold of the fall morning and the warmth of my coat and stocking cap, the rattle of the .22 shells in their box and the anxiety of seeing a moose.

These memories make me earn to go back, but I know that those days can never be again. All I can do is make them happen for my little brother and hope he will see them the same way I did . . . I understand that a lot of things have changed since I was small and that people aren't how they used to be. But that little .22 calibre really brings back a lot of memories.

> We are all storytellers, and our lives are fictions we have made (Rouse, 1978, 12).

SCORES (1-5)

Ideas and content: _____   Word choice: _____

Organization: _____   Sentence fluency: _____

Voice: _____   Conventions: _____

12. SAND DOLLAR

In yestore your, when Moby Dick was a tadpole and the seas rolled and thundered over the jettys and onto the shore. I searched for my first sand doller still hidden somewhere in the ever stretching Silver Beach peninsula.

I'd been going there since a little toddler not finding much more than sea wead and empty crab shells, wich were plucked clean by the screeching sea gulls, nature's best garbage man. Now I was five, I could run and search on my own, no more holding hands with mom and dad. I could run with the big kids down the beach with the wind roaring in my ears like huge jet engines. I was in search of the still fashionable sand doller, that naturally perfect round disc with a dotted star on top and a hole in the center of its flat bottom. While in town the first evening of beachcoming, I spotted just the box I needed for my collection of values to be. It was not just a box, but a red ceder chest approximately 6 by 8 inches and designed like a treasure chest. Mom and dad thought it was just what I needed.

I couldn't wait for morning to come and the night went slow. I could hear the waves beckoning me through the partially open window in my room. Like counting sheep the waves took there toll.

Clam digging started early before light and my parents went clam digging while the tide was still out, and I looked for shells. I found different kinds of shells, broken crabs, empty clams because the sea gulls got to them first, but still no sand dollers.

After lunch mom and dad decided to help me find some sand dollers, but first dad had to stop at a store in Silver Beach.

Dad left me to go ahead and look for sand dollars with mom. When dad got back he helped me to. I was looking up and down, around rocks and in tide pools. Then I spotted it, partially sticking out of the sand, I found It, my first sand doller, It was probably the only one on the beach for 50 miles. I put it in my treasure box with sand still sifty seeping through the hole in the bottom. This shell is in my box besides years of awards, pins and buttons from atheletics and scouting. A shark's tooth from Australia that my Grandpa got for me, and a swiss army knife I found in the woods where I used to live.

These things keep a warm link to my past.

Silver Beach, I found out later didn't have sand dollers, but the local souviner shop kept them In reserve for when Mom and dads would help build up a memory.

SCORES (1-5)

Ideas and content: _____   Word choice: _____

Organization: _____   Sentence fluency: _____

Voice: _____   Conventions: _____

SUGGESTED ANALYTICAL SCORES (PAPERS 1-12)

Paper 1: Making Decisions

Ideas and content: 1-2
Organization: 1-2

Comments: Some readers will disagree with our scores on this piece. It doesn't sound bad when you skim it. It seems to say something, doesn't it? The problem is, it's a compilation of generalizations that do not add up to much of anything. When you are making a decision, look at your choices and be careful. Suppose this writer had described one difficult decision, for example, moving away from home or taking a first job. The writer might have gotten more involved and so might we.

What's missing here is a flesh-and-blood person doing something. There are no people populating this paper. It's sterile. Too much writing of this type (so common in textbooks and educational journals) tends to give the reader a resounding headache. That's because it is stressful to be continually wrestling with big, nebulous concepts, trying to tie them down to something real and familiar. As readers, we get tired. We want out.

Notice the minor conventional problems: "hopefully," the misused semicolon, "effected." Suppose you returned this paper to the writer with just these problems circled in red? What would the message be? What message would *you* want to give this writer?

Paper 2: On the Trail

Ideas and content: 5
Organization: 5

Comments: Here is a simple story, well told. This writer is writing what he knows but from the heart and with total involvement in the text. The organization of this piece is particularly strong. The writer sets the stage by describing the scene, yet without dwelling too much on small details. We get just enough.

Like the sled, this story zips right along, increasing in momentum right up to the top of the hill, then quieting down during the scene with the dogs back in the yard, and during the soft-spoken conclusion. It has a natural pacing and rhythm. Did the writer intend this? Who can say? Anyway, it works. As he writes, he discovers and we discover how terrific these dogs are and how well they fit the land in which they live. There are some problems with conventions but remember, we're not scoring that trait here.

Paper 3: My Watch and My Stereo

Ideas and content: 2
Organization: 1

Comments: Perhaps the moral of this story is, don't try to compare a stereo and a watch, or, more to the point, don't impose artificial structure on your text and hope for organization. We do sometimes try to teach it this way, of course: Have a topic sentence with three supporting details, or a five-paragraph essay with an opening paragraph, three "body" paragraphs, and a summary of those three main points. Why doesn't it work? Because content and organization have to go together; they have to move in rhythm, like dancers. Here, they couldn't be more out of step. The writer cannot really make up her mind, cannot bear to let go of either topic, yet isn't fully involved with either topic. She holds on halfheartedly to both, but this paper isn't a good candidate for the comparison-contrast format, and content suffers. We don't find out as much as we need to know about either gift, and we never really get inside the head of this writer.

Paper 4: Darkness Engulfs Me

Ideas and content: 2-3
Organization: 3
Voice: 3
Word choice: 3-4

Comments: Some papers are, one might say, right on the fringe. This is one of those papers. It almost works, but it doesn't quite come off. Why? It tries too hard, for one thing. It doesn't ring true; it depends too much on clichés, both in language and ideas. The ending disappoints us; the light in the distance is too convenient, like the proverbial dream ending. As readers, we tend to resent the easy way out, and we should.

The paragraphing in this piece is so regular that it almost sets up its own cadence. It has little to do with the true organization, however, which is based on a time sequence, combined with a growing sense of doom about the speaker's future. Unfortunately, we don't quite believe it, and the writer doesn't either, so we don't care as much about this speaker as we feel we should. Our lack of concern makes us uncomfortable. In real life most of us would set this story down and move on to something else. We know it's a student writer, though, so we feel a little guilty about wanting to put it down and look for what works well. It has focus, it doesn't wander, it has a discernible theme, and it makes an effort at characterization. In order to care about what happens in this story, however, we'd have to care more and know more about the protagonist, which might be the place to begin revising.

Paper 5: Special Friend

Ideas and content: 4-5
Organization: 5
Voice: 5
Word choice: 4

Comments: Here is a student who is writing for himself, and the voice comes through loud and clear. Hearing a paper like this one can do more to help build skills than an hour's worth of encouragement to "be yourself" or "write from the heart." This is how writing from the heart sounds, at least in one individual's voice.

There's more good news, too. The writer isn't afraid of the prompt ("Describe a special friend.") but plunges in and gracefully rises above an admittedly lame topic. The pacing is excellent, and the ending is just right; it concludes the piece while leaving us with just a bit of something new. It is an exploration, though we have the feeling that this writer has traveled some of this ground before. This isn't a first draft; it's been kicking around in his head a while. Nevertheless, he manages to retain much of the spontaneous tone. This is spontaneity with a little polish rubbed on, and the effect is pleasing indeed.

Transitions are so smooth that you don't have to think of them. Notice what he does with the "hop, skip, and jump" cliché. We would hope to see more of this in students' writing. Other phrases that have a nice ring: "I wouldn't want to be stuck behind enemy lines with him. . . ."; "Is he my kemosabe?"; "By the way?! Am I nuts??"; ". . . grow old and wise together."

Paper 6: Shoes

Ideas and content: 4
Organization: 4-5
Voice: 5
Word choice: 3-4

Comments: This paper has a forthright, direct tone that is appealing. We have chosen to include it here, though it's really one of those "You-had-to-be-there" pieces. Only if you are part of an analytical scoring team that is reading "favorite object" papers and have just finished reading 200 papers on special rocks, 200 papers on favorite blankets and teddy bears, and another 50 or so papers on special bracelets, bands, and necklaces can you truly appreciate the humor of this piece. Nevertheless, even out of context, the paper has a strong voice.

Some teachers have objected to the "smart-alecky" tone. Frankly, this objection seems to us a little off the mark. The humorous tone is really quite gentle, and the writer seems to poke fun at herself as well as at the prompt; she is only being honest.

Some readers are put off by the fact that, as they see it, this writer gets off rather easily. She wrote a response that, in effect, was no response, and it worked. She got by with something—and this always makes some people uncomfortable. Many people feel that you're supposed to sweat when you write. Don't worry; it probably won't be that simple next time.

Paper 7: Fish Tank

Ideas and content: 4
Organization: 3
Voice: 4
Word choice: 3-4

Comments: This is not a simple paper to score. Sometimes it hovers on the edge of being wonderful, and then it sounds an off-key note that makes us want to hurry on. It is a frustrating paper to read. It's the sort of paper that a teacher will read through several times, hoping to have missed something or hoping to smooth out the text by the act of reading itself.

The ideas are fairly clear: The writer finds a fish tank, thinks how much fun it would be to outfit the tank (instead of taking it to the dump), spends almost more than she can afford in doing so, loses herself in her new hobby, and eventually grows bored with the whole matter. These various shifts in attitude are not well developed.

In fact, the biggest problem with this paper is its lack of transition; we're tossed from point to point with very little solid footing to land on. Inferences are simple to draw, of course; most of us have had a hobby at some time that we tackled with enthusiasm before it became a nuisance. The shift in attitude, not the tank itself, is the real theme of the piece, but the writer is still discovering this. She is still a draft or two away from satisfying herself and us. We have to bring a lot of ourselves to this paper. How much you're willing to bring to it probably has much to do with how you score it and what your response is.

Still, there are some fine moments. The introduction is outstanding, a no-frills beginning that gets right to the heart of the matter. Also appealing: "My mind soon outgrew my pocketbook."; "A weekend getaway type of thing."; "For the time being, it's tolerable."; "The constant buzzing of the pumps rocks me to sleep at night." It's a paper that has a distinctive sound, which is offset by some equally awkward moments: "I had decisions to make about money-matters."; "I had reached a peak in the assessory imagination."; "Little to my knowledge. . . ."

Here, though, which is most encouraging, is a writer who is unafraid to experiment with language, one who clearly enjoys playing with words. If the experiment doesn't always work, the occasional successes still merit some applause.

> It's been a good thing that babies don't understand the concept of "clumsiness" or else they'd never learn to walk (Ziegler, 1981, 19).

Paper 8: Runaway Ralph

Ideas and content: 2

Organization: 1

Voice: 1-2

Word choice: 1-2

Sentence fluency: 2-3

Conventions: 3-4

Comments: Here's a lesson in how to make a few words go a long way. This is a paper that takes one comment—*Runaway Ralph* is a good book—and attempts to make an essay out of it. The paper has only one point to make and makes it relentlessly, never encumbering us with detail.

The organization is especially weak, since the paper begins with an unsupported premise (the only support is the writer's often-repeated opinion) and never leaves the security of that one point in order to branch out into something interesting.

The voice is almost nonexistent, unless you read the piece as a parody, but that would be stretching it. Some raters, citing the writer's apparent enthusiasm, would give this paper a higher score on voice. Again, we think this would be stretching matters. We're not persuaded that under hypnosis this student would actually name the book *Runaway Ralph* as his favorite object. The sentence structure is jarring and irregular. Yet the conventions are handled fairly well. True, there are flaws, but, overall, its use of conventions is its relative strength, though it must be pointed out that the writer attempts nothing very difficult. This paper plays it as "safe" with conventions as with other aspects of the writing.

Paper 9: The Window I Broke

Ideas and content: 2

Organization: 3

Voice: 2

Word choice: 3
Sentence fluency: 3-4
Conventions: 4

Comments: Again, this is a paper in which its use of conventions is its relative strength. Although it's considerably smoother than the paper on *Runaway Ralph,* it doesn't have *much* more in the way of content. The paper is focused, and there is some development. There's also an effort to use the bill for the broken window as an organizational tool, but the connection seems forced, so it doesn't quite work. The title seems misleading, and we feel tricked.

We also don't know much about the broken-window episode, and it would seem that a matchbook from Reggie's might have been a more treasured souvenir. This is a superficial paper in which the writer repeatedly comes close to revealing something about himself, but never quite does. What really happened in the condo? What was so great about Reggie's? He *almost* tells us; he comes painfully close but then thinks better of it and pulls back.

The paper is so starved for details, it's hard to feel convinced that this writer had nearly as good a time as he claims. The clichés deaden what little voice tries to emerge: "It was great. . . ."; "It's fun. . . ."; "really nice"; "major hangouts." There could be a story here, but the writer hasn't found it yet.

Paper 10: What Scares Me

Ideas and content: 2-3
Organization: 2
Voice: 3
Word choice: 3
Sentence fluency: 1-2
Conventions: 2

Comments: Here's an intriguing piece with such an innovative use of parentheses that it's difficult to think of anything else while we are scoring it. We do have a strong sense of the writer here because this writer is not as reserved as some are. She speaks honestly, though the ideas tend to come rapid-fire and to overlap one another, confounding us and leaving us to find our own way out.

The voice would have more power if it did not depend so much upon the writer's intensity and (almost humorous) urgency for its energy. The organization needs work, but there is an effort to impose some structure: It seems to say, "Here is the problem—now, what should we do about it?" More focus and more development would help. There's too much going on in this paper; still, it's a refreshing shift from the paper that says nothing in a dozen different ways.

Sentence structure is the real weakness; the sentences often start in one direction and then head in another. Here is one example: "They are terrorists for the money for other groups, getting mad at something, they might be foreign criminals, their sick, such as mental health, dope, pills, drunk, and sick in the body." Like the ideas themselves, they squirm right out of the writer's control.

There's a lesson to be learned here: More development doesn't mean piling on more ideas. It means skillfully, purposefully connecting ideas that we've thought through and *still* believe.

Paper 11: Survival Rifle

Ideas and content: 4-5

Organization: 3-4

Voice: 5

Word choice: 4

Sentence fluency: 4

Conventions: 4-5

Comments: Normally, repetition is not a strength in building sentences, but in this paper, the cadence, far from being monotonous, gives the paper its driving power: *"I remember. . . . I remember. . . . I remember."* It's so wonderful that the shift at the end of the text is jarring, despite the gentle philosophy about how things change. One of the real frustrations in district-level assessment is having to deal with inconsistencies like these and trying to resolve them with one score. We want to say, "The sentences in the first part of your paper work so very well, but the last part breaks the rhythm." We try to say this with a 4, which of course, isn't enough to convey the message. In the classroom, however, where we might conference with this student, we could convey the message very well; then the score would have meaning.

This paper is so personal and real that the voice cannot help but be strong. Details mesh beautifully. They're well selected, the sort of telling details only the writer could know. The order is a bit arbitrary. We're moved in and out of the cabin more than feels comfortable. Yet, despite this flaw, the central theme—growing up, coming of age— comes through clearly.

Paper 12: Sand Dollar

Ideas and content: 4-5

Organization: 5

Voice: 5

Word choice: 4

Sentence fluency: 4

Conventions: 2

Comments: This writer is doing a lot of things right, but it's hard to appreciate the results during the first reading. Conventions get in the way—less in this typed version than in the original. (The original version contains numerous words that have been crossed out and respelled; the writer works hard to make the message readable.)

This is a paper (one of many) that must be read aloud to be truly enjoyed. Ask a friend to read it to you—preferably someone who reads with some expression and can dance around the faulty punctuation without breaking stride. This is the work of a natural storyteller who, it happens, has difficulty with both spelling and punctuation.

The sentences, nevertheless, gain their strength from diversity and remarkably well constructed transitions. The flow is energetic yet smooth. This writer also has a knack for including not only enough detail but also just the right detail. The paper tells us enough yet never wallows around in trivia.

It opens with a beginning that's almost poetic in its rhythm and that sweeps the reader right along. Then the writer wraps everything up with a conclusion that fits perfectly.

In workshops, invariably someone points out that Moby Dick did not begin life as a tadpole. We're simply not as troubled by this inconsistency as a number of people would like us to be. Furthermore, someone will note, the writer is not *that* old. What right does he have to hearken back to some distant, foggy past? Our only response to this question is that time moves at a markedly different pace for children. When one is thirteen, the distance back to age five is vast, in comparison to, say, forty looking back on thirty-two. It seems that this writer has said just that.

Moreover, this paper isn't really about sand dollars. Like the paper about the address book and the one about the rifle, this paper is about life, about growing up, about seeing things from the other person's point of view, and about learning the value of memories.

It's sometimes said that one of the tests of good literature is that the reader likes it more when returning to it. We've read this paper countless times and like it a little more with each reading.

SUGGESTED ANALYTICAL SCORES FOR HOLISTIC PRACTICE PAPERS

Following are suggested analytical scores for the six holistic papers that were given in the first part of this chapter. (If you want more practice, you might go back and score any or all of these papers analytically before you look at the following scores.)

PAPER A: NEW ORLEANS

Ideas and content: 2
Organization: 2
Voice: 3-4
Word choice: 3
Sentence Fluency: 3
Conventions: 2

PAPER B: MY ADDRESS BOOK

Ideas and content: 5
Organization: 5
Voice: 5
Word choice: 5
Sentence Fluency: 4
Conventions: 4

PAPER C: SPOON COLLECTION

Ideas and content: 2-3
Organization: 3-4
Voice: 3
Word choice: 3-4
Sentence fluency: 3-4
Conventions: 3-4

PAPER D: GUNS

Ideas and content: 2
Organization: 1
Voice: 2-3
Word choice: 3
Sentence fluency: 2
Conventions: 2-3

PAPER E: THE PAST

Ideas and content: 1-2
Organization: 1-2
Voice: 2

Word choice: 2-3

Sentence fluency: 2-3

Conventions: 2

PAPER F: THE COAT
Ideas and content: 4

Organization: 4

Voice: 4-5

Word choice: 3-4

Sentence fluency: 4

Conventions: 3-4

IF YOUR SCORES DON'T AGREE

Don't be too concerned if your scores don't agree with ours, but do have good reasons for scoring as you did. Our scores (which are based on our own impressions as well as on those of other trained professional raters) result from several careful readings of each paper and from discussion of the paper with other teachers.

We believe the scores are valid and justifiable, and we've tried to indicate some of our reasons in the comments following each piece. Nevertheless, these scores are impressions and cannot be more. You may have an additional or even conflicting perspective on any or all of the papers, which is *also* valid and adds to the total "truth" about any given paper. If possible, read the papers with a colleague and compare your results; then look at your scores in light of the suggested scores just given. When your scores are (1) defensible; (2) capable of being articulated; and (3) tied to explicit written criteria (those in this book or your own), they will be useful to you and to your student writers.

POSTSCRIPT

If writing assessment has taught us anything, it's that students *can* write. Nearly every paper shows a hint of promise. There are a remarkable few that show much more. Those of us who write a lot and who know what it takes to pull the writing together have acquired a profound respect for what many students are able to do under the admitted constraints of assessment: limited time, an assigned topic, and so forth. Here, from numerous impressive performances that we have seen over the years, are two we wish to share with you.

SOME THINGS DO NOT CHANGE

by Peter Hawkinson, Age 17

Jacob Warner poured milk over his corn flakes. Remarkable, he thought, that they had not changed at all in the last hundred years or so. Sometimes he would spend the whole morning with his corn flakes. He liked to think of them as a link with his past, a past nobody under age one-sixty or so remembered. Yes, he concluded, Corn Flakes are okay. And he lapsed into nostalgia.

He had met Marsha at a political rally back in 2017. The candidate was Thomas Cruise, running for his second term in the U.S. Senate. Old Tom Cruise movies were being viewed with the same tongue-in-cheek malice as old Reagan films had been back when Jacob was in college.

When Marsha's eyes met his from across the room, he was in his twenty-fourth year of being age twenty-nine. They had fallen in love, and lived together for three years. He had always meant to tell her he was immortal. He had even toyed with the idea of reproducing the accident for her benefit. Before he could do either, Marsha's GM/Toyota Starburst wrapped itself around a streetlamp. GM/Toyota . . . antithesis . . . Naoko.

Naoko was a vice president at GM/T. He met her at a trade convention in '31 back when he was freelancing as an aerodynamics engineer. She was interested in hiring him to help design a new airdam system. Soon, they both became interested in much more. What a woman she was, underneath the 3-piece suit. An apartment at the top of Tokyo . . . strings gently plucking out an ancient Oriental folk song . . . Osake . . . and, through the rice paper screens, moonlight.

Walking on the moon was just like the old Police song described it. When Naoko succumbed to Superflu in '37, Jacob had been quarantined on the moon. It wasn't so bad . . . a free trip to space, a chance to explore the surface in places the guided tours don't go, and a beautiful view of the earth. He hadn't worried about the Superflu. Immortals simply don't get sick. They just move on down . . . on down the road . . . on down under.

Which brought him to Sydney. From there, he went on foot into the Outback. Government protection had put a halt to industrialization of the region in 1993. The Aborigines were still there, still living as they had for centuries. It was the perfect life—digging for grubs, hunting kangaroos, and by the fire each night, sharing the Dreamtime legends. He stayed there for fully eighty years. When he left, the natives honored him with his own legend—"He who did not age." They were the only people he ever stayed with long enough for them to guess his secret. They were the only people he felt deserving of his trust. But he was changing their lives too much; a white man in their midst just wouldn't do if they were to keep their culture pure. He moved on. Went to New York. Started acting. Ate a lot of Corn Flakes.

He looked down at the bowl. The Corn Flakes were soggy. Glancing at his wristwatch, he realized he'd been lost in memories for two hours. Well, he snorted, I've got a hell of a lot to remember. Too much for one man. One hundred and sixty-four years of life doesn't leave much undone. And it still wasn't enough time to change Corn Flakes. Some things just don't change. A Corn Flake is still a Corn Flake, and a man's life is still the sum of his memories and his experiences. He figured he had only one experience left.

He put the Corn Flakes into the refrigerator. Maybe someone would eat them later. And the world's first and last immortal human being put the pistol into his mouth and fired.

This paper received all 5s from both raters (teachers) who scored it. It has grace, style, wit, and exceptional control, particularly from such a young writer. Like everyone, I have personal biases that often get in the way of fair evaluation. I tend to like stories about baseball, horses, the wilderness, family relationships; I tend not to like science fiction at all. This paper changed my mind, at least temporarily. It's smooth, developed, extraordinarily well paced and entertaining—the work of a gifted writer.

Peter's Comments

Recently, after reading the paper for the first time since he had written it several years ago, Peter added these comments:

In hindsight, my skill as a writer peaked right around the time of this story. At that point, I was writing creatively upwards of two hours each day, and sharing my work via computer modem with other writers in the Portland area.

As for the story behind the story: The piece was written during forty-five minute English periods on three consecutive days. The concept at work, "Some things never change," was one of three allowable themes. The original idea was for Jacob Warner to be an immortal Supreme Court Justice (he gets appointed to a lifetime position, and remains ageless through countless administrations and confounds a lot of politicians), but I changed my mind on the second day. It didn't make sense; nobody would want to do the same thing for a hundred years. It came to me, as the deadline approached, that Jacob should make a statement about living a full life by killing himself. I had only to show that his life was full. The memories I threw together from all over. I made the obligatory futuristic references to modern institutions. A friend of mine fell in love with a Naoko while in Japan. I had been reading a book of Dreamtime legends the night before. Corn Flakes have been around at breakfast all my life. I just threw it all together . . .

JEFF

by Carolyn Stacey, Age 17

I knew that Jeff was downstairs and that the light wasn't on. His bag would have been a formless shape crouching at his feet. I supposed the train still traveled in his mind and that his thoughts were slowly untangling to form coherence. Nevertheless, I made no move to aid him, and lay silently studying the wall.

No one had welcomed his arrival. The smeared letter still lay accusingly behind the couch. Days before, my father roamed the house like a misplaced nomad, his anger audible in quick, heavy snorts of breath. Mother was worse. She carried her fury and self-hate to work and fired three administrators in two days. They sat sullenly in the evenings, both hoping that the other would take Jeff's photograph down from the mantel where it sat with his acceptance to Bennington and my music trophies.

Conversation was obsolete, as was any communication between them and me. The friends who already knew came over to defend him, but left hurriedly—one with imprints of a poker on his right shoulder.

I think that my parents resented the fact that his friends had left this loathsome secret for us to discover. They were vile accomplices to a major crime—slimy representations of the ultimate sin. Unknowing, they all left with the name "Faggot" engraved upon their reputations.

Now, when introduced to a new male companion of mine, my parents coldly regard him and dismiss us. I feel the blame becoming an impossible weight that suffocates my dreams and my love for them.

I still think of him as Jeff. He is the only owner of that name; all others are pretenders and plagiarists. I never utter it at home, succumbing to rules sprung from fear and defeat.

And that night, as his soundless tears slid endlessly down his profile illuminated by the streetlight, I drew the covers nearer to me. My parents' breathing created a rhythmic rustling down the hallway and for one sickening moment I hoped to hear it cease. But it continued, bearing up the dark, and I let mine join theirs.

This paper, like Peter Hawkinson's paper, received all 5s from both raters (teachers) who scored it in the district assessment. It is remarkable in its combination of subtlety and frankness. The text creates a strong sense of tension with its theme of suppressed anger that threatens to burst in many directions but is constantly reburied, a little deeper each time. Anyone who has felt emotionally distanced from another person can identify with the paper on some level, but,

ultimately, it works simply because the writer manages, in a very short time, to make us care about what happens.

These phrases stand out most for me: ". . . the train still traveled in his mind. . . ."; ". . . lay accusingly behind the couch."; ". . . my father roamed the house like a misplaced nomad. . . ."; ". . . others are pretenders and plagiarists."; ". . . it continued, bearing up the dark." The words are striking, and they're borne along in graceful, fluid sentences whose easy rhythm belies yet somehow reinforces the somber tone of this piece.

If the paper has a weakness—and it's a small one—it's the digression, to the story of the friends, who seem as intrusive in the paper as in the story it recounts, but the ending makes up for this digression. It's an ending that refuses to take the easy way out by making everything all right. We try with our thoughts to push the writer up, out of bed, and down the stairs. She will not go. This is a writer who makes her own choices—and she is right.

In Closing

Over the years, we who have been privileged to score student papers have taught ourselves invaluable lessons about *writing* through the process of *evaluation.* You can do this too. We hope you will continue to score student papers and to discuss the results with colleagues so that you can learn from one another. We also hope you will teach students to evaluate writing so that they can be in on this important part of the writing process.

3

HOLISTIC AND ANALYTICAL ASSESSMENT: SOME COMPARISONS

- *My story was short but meaningful.*
- *Most people are too accustomed to living to want to die.*
- *They are our next store neighbors.*
- *I think Doug should be psychotic, he's so good with advice.*
- *The other team's coach was yelling obscene gestures.*
- *Life is just one survival after another.*
- *Unlike most, my father became bald at twenty-one. This enabled him to become athletically inclined.*
- *"Up and Adams," he whispered.*
- *Challenges are breath-taking and sweat-dripping.*
- *He wasn't God, but he was very talented.*
- *My favorite sweeter is my UCLA sweeter.*
- *Old foggies are people that togetherness means a lot.*
- *She was 4'10" tall before her sudden death.*
- *I love my horse and I'm not going to sell him till he dies.*

Now that you've had a chance to try both holistic and analytical scoring, we'll offer some brief comparisons between them, review some common sources of bias in scoring papers, and offer some suggestions for teaching scoring to student writers in the classroom. Let's begin with some comparisons.

HOLISTIC ASSESSMENT: ADVANTAGES AND PITFALLS

Advocates of holistic assessment often say that it "feels right" because it offers a way in which to see how all the traits work in harmony. Specifically, they point to these advantages:

At the district level, it's cheaper than other methods. Holistic assessment is the least expensive way that we know of to analyze students' writing samples because it's the fastest way. It's important to point out, however, that this apparent cost effectiveness can be overstated.

Time in assessment is eaten up by training raters, preparing exercises, collecting papers, reading the samples (you have to read through it, no matter how you score it), and reporting the results. Virtually all time costs are the same for both holistic and analytical assessment, except the time required to score, record, and report results. Analytical scoring takes a little more time, as you may have noted yourself, but not much more time. It's often claimed that raters can be trained to score a paper holistically in as little as 30 seconds. This is fast, all right—rather alarmingly so. How much thought would go into scoring a paper in such a short period of time? Not much. Very strong and very weak papers may get accurate readings under such a system, but the time required to sort out the weak from the strong may not be there. A careful reading during holistic assessment will still take one to two minutes per paper (based on one- and two-page papers); careful reading during analytical assessment can take as little as two-and-a-half to three minutes per paper. (These rates are for practiced readers; don't be surprised if you are reading at a considerably slower rate.) So, although we acknowledge that holistic assessment *is* the faster method, we have to be careful in analyzing the relative merits of the two in terms of cost.

Holistic assessment encourages readers to look at the "whole" piece, not to segment the writing in some artificial manner. Writing, like cooking, requires an effective blending of skills and ingredients. Holistic assessment recognizes this and fights hard against the isolation of traits, even in analysis. On the other hand, if your apple pie doesn't turn out as expected, it's sometimes helpful to know whether you overbaked it or just left out the spices. Holistic scoring tells us how everything worked together, but tells us next to nothing about *why* a paper did or did not succeed.

Readers gain confidence more rapidly by using holistic assessment than by using other methods. Holistic assessment is easy to understand and to teach at one level. However, as you may have sensed when you did some practice scoring in the preceding chapter, true holistic assessment is anything but simple. Because it demands attention to many factors at one time, it requires a very sophisticated integration of skills. In holistic assessment, a rater must consider a range of traits but come up with only *one* score that reflects performance across all of these traits—a task that looks simple but isn't.

Here are some potential pitfalls of holistic assessment:

Audiences may find that results are less useful than they had hoped. This is not an inherent fault of holistic assessment. Rather, it is a result of using holistic assessment for the wrong purposes—for example, to obtain diagnostic information. Holistic data provide only general information about students' performances, so to expect more is to invite disappointment. As we've noted already, holistic assessment is most useful for making decisions involving placement or selection, not those requiring diagnosis of strengths and weaknesses.

Biases may be simple to mask. Holistic scores aren't always very holistic in reality. A single score can be an effective camouflage for a host of biases. What does the score truly represent: the paper as a whole, the rater's response to conventions, ideas, or handwriting? Sometimes it's difficult to say which of these it represents. Of course, analytical scores also can be influenced by biases.

A single score provides no means of reflecting relative strengths and weaknesses. Holistic scores tend to suggest that papers are altogether wonderful, mediocre, or wretched. In fact, this is only sometimes the case. Often, papers are wonderful in some respects but less wonderful in others. Writers need to know which areas are which.

Nevertheless, if we specify criteria, carefully select anchor papers, and carefully train raters, we can achieve a valid and reliable overall index of students' writing proficiency. While such scores are of limited value in the classroom because of their unfocused nature, they can serve some purposes. For instance, you could gather a sample of students' writing at the beginning of the year, select anchor papers, and score holistically. Then you could file the exercise, the anchor papers, and the scores. At the end of the year, you could repeat the assessment, scoring the end-of-year papers *using the beginning-of-the-year anchor papers.* A comparison of students' scores between the beginning and the end of the year would reveal some information about the impact of your writing instruction. (Incidentally, this same analysis could be carried out by using analytical score scales.)

Furthermore, you could repeat the same writing assessment, using the same exercise and the same anchor papers at the beginning of each school year as a quick evaluation of the starting point of each group of students. By holding the anchor papers constant over the years, you could see where each group stood, in terms of general, overall writing skills, in relation to previous students.

ANALYTICAL ASSESSMENT: ADVANTAGES AND PITFALLS

Advocates of analytical assessment, who tend to feel that writing is just too complex to be summed up by means of one score, often point out the following advantages:

Analytical assessment provides a means of reflecting the relative strengths and weaknesses in a given piece of writing. This statement is true. Furthermore, when scores are aggregated within a building or across a district or state, some trends may be spotted. It may be, for example, that students in one classroom, building, or district demonstrate relative strengths in ideas and voice, while those in another classroom show more control over sentences and conventions.

Teachers who participate as readers derive in-service benefits from the experience of analytical assessment because they learn ways of analyzing students' writing that they can use in the classroom and can teach to students. Of course, there are in-service benefits in holistic assessment, too, but teachers often feel that analytical assessment comes closer to providing the kind of analysis that students need as a foundation for revision.

Because it demands development of a written scoring guide (which may or may not be used in holistic assessment), analytical assessment encourages readers to come to grips with what they value in a piece of writing. By committing those values to paper, raters (teachers) create a working vocabulary with which to talk intelligently about writing.

Analytical assessment recognizes the importance of voice, provided this is one of the traits defined in the scoring guide. Holistic assessment may, of course, encompass voice. When a single score is given, however, it is very easy for the scoring to lean toward an evaluation of "correctness." Even if this doesn't happen, a paper with strong voice but weak conventions will usually receive no more than a mediocre score in holistic assessment. When the writers get their papers back, they may very well interpret this type of score as meaning, "Your writing didn't work." Sometimes a more useful, and more accurate, message is, "Your story moved me, but it needs polishing." Analytical assessment can provide this kind of message.

Analytical assessment also has some pitfalls. Some of them are as follows:

At the building or district level, analytical assessment can be very expensive if it isn't well managed. As we've indicated, two- or three-page papers can be scored analytically within three to four minutes, but it could easily take longer, especially when readers are very conscientious.

On the other hand, it's a myth that a paper will need to be read six times if it's to receive six scores. Analytical raters generally read a paper once and (after the first day or so) rapidly learn to internalize the scoring guide in order to score various traits simultaneously. The real time and expense are taken up by the development of a sound scoring guide, which brings us to a second pitfall.

Criteria and traits must be well defined if they are to yield a sound profile of student performance. A scoring guide that's too skimpy to provide a comprehensive picture of writing performance or so lengthy that it's redundant and cumbersome will not work well. Further, if traits are not well defined, raters may actually be scoring very different sorts of things. Let's say that you're scoring the trait of *ideas.* What is this trait? Focus? Development? Originality? A combination of these? How will raters recognize good or weak performance? The scoring guide must be *very* explicit in answering these questions, or scores will be meaningless.

Putting together a complete, specific scoring guide is a time-consuming, laborious process, and, if it's done right, it's expensive. Not everyone is willing to spend the time, money, and good will to do it. By contrast, finding anchor papers to support a holistic scoring process is a simple, routine task; no wonder holistic scoring has been more popular with districts.

Beginners may feel frustrated with the complexity of the process. Analytical assessment cannot be mastered in a matter of minutes. If you're in a hurry, this isn't a method for you. It takes time (a day of practice, at least, preferably more) and concentration. Learning to separate word choice from voice or organization from ideas is tricky at first, but those raters who stick with it generally feel that it teaches them a great deal about writing. By contrast, holistic scoring feels so much simpler. As we've noted, however, while it's easy to offer a personal impression, true holistic assessment that encompasses a wide range of traits takes extraordinary concentration and skill.

FINAL COMPARISON

Both scoring methods have pluses and minuses. The "right" method depends on your purpose for scoring the papers. Do you want a general idea about which students are having problems or about how well students are writing overall? Then holistic assessment will provide this information. Do you want diagnostic information about specific kinds of strengths and weaknesses, either for individual students or for groups of students? Then analytical assessment will work better for you.

In addition, as we shall show in later chapters, analytical assessment provides excellent support for classroom instruction. It encourages students to think and to talk about writing. It provides a potential structure for those forms of interim assessment already inherent within the writing process, such as peer review and conferencing. It also offers guidelines on which to base revisions, thereby encouraging self-assessment and putting responsibility for assessment where it belongs: in the hands of the writer.

SOME COMMON CAUSES OF RATER BIAS

The following are the major causes of rater bias in holistic or analytical writing assessment. As you were rating the papers in Chapter 2, you may have noticed that some of these factors were affecting your scores:

1. *The positive-negative leniency error.* This is a tendency that some raters have to be too hard or too easy on everyone. Realistic standards that are high enough but are still within reach of students are the order of the day.

2. *The trait error.* Some raters attend heavily to one trait (such as conventions) while ignoring or skimming over others. This can be a problem for either holistic or analytical raters.

3. *Appearance.* How does the paper tend to look at first glance? Handwriting and neatness are not indicators of writing skill but are often treated as if they were. Because you were considering typed samples in Chapter 2, you didn't need to worry very much about appearance, but, usually, this is among the primary causes of rater bias.

4. *Length.* Is longer better? Not necessarily. Is brevity a virtue? Sometimes it is, but at other times it is just a sign of nothing to say. Few beginning writers can write a paper in a paragraph, though now and again a writer pulls it off. Even fewer can sustain powerful writing for more than a page or two. Longer papers may be intermittently wonderful, which makes them harder to score than papers that are consistently good or poor.

5. *Fatigue.* Everybody gets tired. Tired raters skim. Scoring sessions should be kept short, and breaks should be frequent. Classroom teachers who use systematic assessment to evaluate students' writing will, naturally, be setting their own schedules. Most will find that they can assess about twenty to thirty papers per hour holistically, about ten to twenty per hour analytically, depending on length, complexity of the papers, number of traits scored, and a host of other factors.

6. *The personality clash.* Maybe to the writer a motorcycle symbolizes freedom and individuality, while to the rater it signifies irresponsibility, disdain for authority, and mindless rebellion. What winds up being scored—the paper on the cross-country trip to Baja or the student's choice of topic? Raters can also try too hard to compensate for a bias that they know influences their scoring, for example, "I know I hate motorcycle papers, so I'll automatically kick all the scores up a point." In large-scale assessment, it's better to let someone else score the paper if the bias is strong. The classroom teacher, who usually doesn't have this luxury, must simply attempt not to be unduly influenced.

7. *The repetition factor.* "Oh, this paper is just like the last fifty. . . . ," some raters may say to themselves. The more papers raters have to score, the more they confront boredom. Imagine having 100,000 papers to score (as some state assessments do)!

It's hard to be fair when the papers all begin to look and sound alike. Often, the nature of the topic itself invites this sort of mindless repetition: "Write a paper on the sights, sounds, and smells of the beach." How many ways are there to do this? Well before the fiftieth recounting of crashing waves, salty spray, screeching gulls, and lingering sunsets, it ought to occur to us that if we want writing that is personal and original, we must let students choose topics that are personal and original.

8. *Skimming.* Reading every word every time becomes tedious. Doesn't the first paragraph usually tell the story anyhow? The answer is no. Students' writing can undergo a drastic personality change (and sometimes several changes) partway through a paper. We have to try to stay with them.

9. Error of central tendency. If you use an odd-numbered (e.g., 5-point) scoring scale, beware of using the middle of the scale as a midpoint "dumping ground." In other words, be careful not to assign 3s because you're tired and can no longer tell whether a paper is good or not. If you hit this point, it's time for a break.

Some people advocate using an even-numbered (4- or 6-point) scale to avoid the midpoint "dumping ground." Forcing papers up (to 4s) or down (to 2s) when they don't deserve these scores is just as artificial as "dumping" too many in the middle. Whatever scoring scale you use, keep many sample papers on hand, so that you can remind yourself now and again how papers at various scoring levels read.

10. *Self-scoring.* Are you a perceptive reader? If so, be careful that you aren't scoring yourself as a rater or scoring your own ability to decipher

the paper's meaning, to solve the puzzle, rather than rating the writer's skill. Reading is an interactive process, and you must bring something of yourself to any text in order to interpret or to appreciate it, but the writer should be meeting you at least halfway.

11. *Discomfort with the role.* It's hard to make judgments sometimes. Remember that you are rating the paper—and a single performance at that—not the student and not the student's writing talent in general. Nice people do not all write well, and obnoxious people are often annoyingly talented.

12. *The sympathy score.* You may feel that the student "had a tough day," "was really trying," "was doing the best he could," and so forth. Don't score out of sympathy. "Oh, he sounds just like my son!" If you do, you detract from the value of the high score given to another student's performance. Further, student writers cannot be expected to respect scores that are inaccurate.

Some Questions to Ask Yourself

1. Are you easily persuaded? If so, be careful in scoring ideas; you may have a tendency to score too high on this trait.

2. Do you have a need for order? Do you have color-coordinated closets? Do you rip outdated address cards from your Rolodex? People with a great need for order tend to find order in anything and score slightly high on organization. Conversely, if chaos feels natural to you, you may have a difficult time perceiving order even when the writer has worked hard to put it there.

3. How do you react to profanity, vulgar or explicit language, or violence? Some raters have a very ho-hum attitude, while others are put off by these characteristics. It's a good idea for those coordinating a district or state assessment to discuss this ahead of time (especially if they're scoring papers at grade 9 and above) and to decide how to deal with it. There are no right or wrong answers here; each group of raters must decide.

Perhaps the best advice is this: Ask whether the language works in the context of the text. Profanity, for instance, can seem natural and realistic in a war story about Vietnam veterans; or it can sound artificial, irritating, or overdone in a piece on pet goldfish. Not everyone agrees with this perspective, and, furthermore, some people have such a negative reaction to vulgar language that they cannot judge its effectiveness in writing objectively. Professional writers, of course, can get by with a lot, but there's often an inherent expectation on the part of teachers that students should write differently. Should they? What do you think?

4. How much do you think you're influenced by knowing the writer's sex? Perhaps everyone is influenced somewhat. Because some assessment specialists believe there's a slight tendency to score papers

differently when raters know the writer's sex, there's a case to be made for keeping names off papers. The counterargument is that raters can tell anyway—by the handwriting or by contextual clues (use of names or what the writer says). Often raters *can* tell or *think* they can and wish they couldn't. This is a difficult situation to resolve.

5. Do you know the writer? In large-scale assessment, we tell raters not to score papers written by students whom they know because bias is inevitable. If you're using assessment at the building or classroom level, however, this isn't always possible or even desirable. There's great value in comparing your evaluation of your own students with that of another teacher. You can do this by scoring samples of papers in teams across two or more classrooms.

6. What's your pet peeve? Some of us have many. We'll share two of ours. The first is the large, loopy-style writing that fills the entire space between lines and in which all vowels, together with the letter *s*, are indistinguishable one from the other. The second is science fiction writing in which characters whose names we can neither pronounce nor remember use weapons we cannot picture to commit unconscionable yet somehow boring atrocities upon one another.

Some people are so proud of their pet peeves that they don't like the idea of giving them up, even temporarily. Pet peeves get in the way of fair scores, however. Here are the pet peeves that teachers themselves have cited most often over the years.

Repetitive sentence beginnings

Lack of organization

Sentences that end in prepositions; also the sentence, "Where's it at?"

Inappropriate use of "it's" and "its"

Messiness

Carelessness

Run-on sentences

Poor penmanship

Sentence fragments

Rambling on and on

Wordiness

Empty words meant to "snow" the reader or to impress rather than to communicate

"You know what I mean"

Dirty, messy, coffee-stained papers

Tiny writing

Scrawly writing

Writing that is too light

Hard-to-read writing

Papers that close with "The End"

The copout ending: "Then I woke up and it was all a dream. . . ."

Long, contrived strings of adjectives

Apparent lack of sincerity

"Alot"

No side margins

Lack of paragraphing

Lack of voice

Lack of honesty

Safe, boring papers

Random pronouns

Total absence of capitals

". . . and then we . . . , and then we . . . , and then . . . , and then . . . ," or "one month later" in place of detail

". . . and then I pulled out my .357 and blew them away" as a solution to every conflict

Holding back

Lack of originality

Tangled, jumbled sentences

Weak verbs

Beginning sentences with "And"

Beginning sentences with "But"

Confusion

Telling the reader what to think

Repeated errors following revision

"Cuz"

Identical rough drafts and final drafts

Writing with no heart

Do you recognize some of your own pet peeves here? We do, and we also recognize a few things that we're guilty of as writers (not all of which we plan to change).

In the classroom, these pet peeves are less likely to influence scores or grades if we simply take time to be aware of them and even admit them honestly to students. You might ask students to list their own pet peeves, too. Compare their responses to yours and keep a growing list. Post it somewhere. Such a list can teach all of us something about the way we respond to writing.

4

ASSESSMENT AND THE WRITING PROCESS

- *Just like my friend my skirt will go with anything.*
- *Best of all, when Frankie holds onto my nose, I feel very special.*
- *In this composition, I will describe her utmost inner qualities.*
- *I am embarrassed to be related to someone who can't match their clothes and doesn't do their hair every morning.*
- *I like writing S. A.s because you have to write a lot.*
- *Phil was small for his size.*
- *Irma has taught me quite a few stuff.*
- *If I was going to make a change, it would be something worthwild.*
- *I got my bravery and opened it.*
- *I was taken to the hospital emergency room to have my knee relocated.*
- *This is such a vast topic, and due to the fact I'm not being graded on this, I won't get too deep.*
- *My nose is like the black sheep of my face.*
- *More and more elderly are created each day.*
- *I could feel knowledge rush upon me.*

So much has been written about "the writing process" during the past several years that you might easily get the idea there is *a* writing process or a single correct model that everyone should follow. However, it's more useful—and more correct—to suppose that there's a general philosophy underlying the writing process approach that in practice can take many different forms. (Unfortunately, this is not always the way the writing process is presented to students in practice.)

Given the abundance of excellent texts on this topic, we will not belabor explanations of the process itself. The purpose of this chapter is to show how and where assessment can fit into the process by focusing particularly on teacher comments, peer review, revision, and conferencing—four components in which assessment can play a key role.

If assessment (particularly self-assessment) is going to work effectively within the writing process, then it's important that the process itself not be too rigid, too bound by time limits and other artificial constraints. In short, the process must serve the student writers, not the reverse, and management of the process must, to the extent possible, be put in the hands of the student writers. This is so because writers do not all work the same way or at the same speed.

PROS AND CONS OF THE PROCESS APPROACH TO WRITING

Initially, the process approach to writing was an attempt to escape the traditional, more structured approach to writing that many of us grew up with: "For Monday, write 500 words about a person who has influenced your life." What happened between the Friday assignment and the Monday turning in of papers was largely the writer's own business. It was mostly (or sometimes wholly) unsupervised. It was often chaotic. It was frequently mysterious, both to the writer and to everyone else. Most depressing of all, it was often ineffective—but not for everyone.

Some students always seemed to be able to write about anything, anywhere, anytime with little or no assistance. How did they do it? Was it genius, perseverance, luck? Whatever it was, those students emerged as writers. Gradually, the rest of us began asking what it was they were doing that was different. The result of many attempts to answer this question has somewhat loosely converged into what we now generically term "the writing process."

THE WRITING PROCESS: SOME SPECIFICS

Not everyone talks about the writing process in exactly the same way. In fact, if you attend two different seminars on the writing process, chances are that the transparencies and handouts will look sufficiently different to give you the vaguely disquieting feeling that somebody has gotten part of it wrong. The real differences, though, are usually just a matter of emphasis (more prewriting, less revision) or of terminology. Generally, the traditional steps within the writing process include the following:

Prewriting
Drafting
Revising
Polishing and editing
Publishing (or sharing)
Evaluating (or assessing)

The process, or the movement from step to step, is taken to be cyclical and recursive, meaning that we can move in either direction, perhaps forward from prewriting to drafting, then backward to prewriting, and then forward again through drafting and revising.

Furthermore, each step can take many shapes and forms. One writer's "prewriting," for instance, may look very different from what other writers do. Moreover, some writers may spend hours, days or even weeks prewriting and doing research, while others start right in. Similarly, some writers revise endlessly, but not all do so. Writers need their own timetables, their own ways of collecting and processing information, and their own versions of the writing process.

Steps within the writing process are not only recursive but overlapping as well. In Figure 4.1 the steps look clean and discrete, like boxcars in a train. (Graphics, like text, can tell lies.) *Some* prewriting and drafting occur during revision, for instance. Some revision may occur in the writer's head before the writer even picks up a pencil. Revision and editing, for the experienced writer, are inextricably mixed.

The writing process is often presented in a way that suggests writing is simple and systematic. This, of course, is reductive and misleading. In truth, writing is an extraordinarily complex task, much of which occurs inside the writer's head. It's a mistake, therefore, to suppose that the how-to's of writing can be summed up like a recipe for bran muffins.

Writers do a great deal of writing by instinct and some of it by chance. So, in learning to write, you must discriminate: Take what's useful from the writing process and pitch the rest. What works for one writer won't work for everyone every time, and some things may not work for some writers at all. Forcing student writers to brainstorm for ten minutes every time they write or to spend hours revising what they already feel comfortable and satisfied with is just as artificial as insisting that a paper about an influential person be exactly 500 words long. Every approach to writing has its own potential for tyranny.

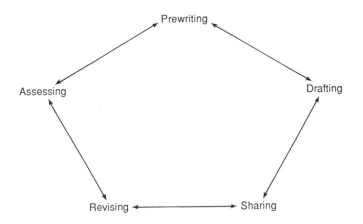

FIGURE 4.1. Writing Process

Further, writers do not write the very same way every time—nor should they, for that matter. On some days, ideas flow easily, and on other days—nothing. Yes, we know. Prewriting is supposed to loosen up the mental gears and get things humming again. If this works for you (as a *writer*, not as a teacher), then we say fine; we'll take your word for it. But sometimes prewriting can be more annoying than helpful.

This is not to say that activities such as brainstorming, networking, clustering, listing, and so forth should not be part of a student's repertoire. They should be. We make a mistake, however, when we hope that such activities will work like a magic potion and will take the place of experience or forge connections that the writer neither sees nor feels yet.

Making connections is what writing is all about. When the topic is close to the heart, an activity like clustering, mapping, or networking may be all that's needed to start the threads intertwining. At other times, only writing itself will do the job, for in drafting, the writer reshapes ideas, sees what's missing, raises questions, and—most important—not only sees the connections that are there but also actually *expresses the nature of those connections.*

Drafting sentences and connecting one whole thought to another requires a deeper level of thinking than does brainstorming. That's why it's harder. Prewriting techniques like brainstorming can trick student writers into thinking that writing is easy. It is not. We write not only to discover what we know but also to discover what we do *not* yet know.

Allowing student writers to select and to define their own topics is an important—perhaps the *most* important—starting point in making the writing process serve the writer. It's often hard for us to do this. We have so many "important" questions we want answered. Ask a group of young writers to respond to a global topic like "World Peace," and the responses you'll get, almost without exception, will be hopelessly dull, banal, circular, and general: "My idea of world peace would be a world in which there was no war and no violence—just everybody loving everybody all the time." What's wrong here? Hasn't this writer clustered enough? No, that isn't it. She hasn't *lived* enough, hasn't *experienced* enough to condense this vaporous topic into writing that is substantial and heartfelt. At the global level she has little to say, and who can blame her? Topics like "World Peace" are the sprawly, shapeless, amorphous stuff of which political speeches are made.

Part of the problem, of course, is that this isn't *her* topic at all but someone else's. To say her writing lacks focus, specificity, and originality is to miss the point. The point is that she *has nothing to say to us on this subject*—at least not yet. Her response is a kind of prethinking on paper. If we step in now and assess her work, we do her and ourselves an injustice. Before this writer can produce anything it makes sense to assess, she needs time to write more, read her writing aloud, pose some questions she can't answer yet, talk them through with other writers, hear their writing, read what published writers have said about the topic, respond to their writing, integrate, and then redefine the topic in a way she can handle.

> Writers need their own topics. Right from the first day of kindergarten students should use writing as a way to think about and give shape to their own ideas and concerns (Atwell, 1987, 117).

We have learned that writers need an opportunity to rethink and revise, but if we impose on student writers a *mechanized version* of the writing process, we may take away the very opportunity we seek to provide. If we brainstorm on Monday, draft on Tuesday, revise on Wednesday, and edit on Thursday, can we publish on Friday? Not necessarily. It isn't this simple or this clean, and we mustn't encourage student writers (or teachers) to think that it is, or they'll feel that they're failing all the time. Writing is sometimes easy and joyful, of course, but it's usually difficult, frustrating, messy, disjointed, and very time consuming. The purpose of the writing process isn't to take all the pain and sweat out of writing or to reduce it to six neat steps; the real purpose of the writing process is to give student writers time, space, and freedom in which to write and to offer them a repertoire of skills from which they can pick and choose in teaching themselves to write, for in the end, this is what every writer does.

> Writers need regular chunks of time —time to think, write, confer, read, change their minds, and write some more. . . . Writers need time to write well (Atwell, 1987, 118).

Writing and Revising

Within the writing process model *writing* is usually taken to be the umbrella term, of which *revising* is one central component. This is one way of looking at things, and it's a comfortable model that follows logically from the way writing has generally been taught: We write, then we revise (whatever that is), then we write some more, and, finally, we edit and polish, if it's a piece that we plan to publish or to share in some formal way.

Perhaps it's more realistic, though—from the real writer's perspective—to say that *revision* is the proper umbrella term, of which writing is one component (revision in the sense of "revisioning" or "rethinking" one's ideas). In other words, the heart of the writing process is what goes on in the writer's head—the mental part, the thinking part. Putting the words on paper—the writing part—is a component of working and reworking the vision, which emerges in some form that can be shared with others or preserved for the writer. Having said this, we're in a somewhat better position to see how assessment, or evaluation, fits within the writing process. It's easier to think through ideas when you can see them in front of you in written form. However, if we're going to use writing to help us to think, we can see why it's important not to jump in too soon and to judge the quality of what only *looks* to be the "final product" but is really the writer's thinking in process.

We can also see that *much* of assessment, like writing and revising, is mental. We can sometimes assess without pen in hand. The word *assessment* puts some people off because it sounds too much like testing. What we really mean is *review*; perhaps this is a more palatable and, in some ways, more accurate term. Call it *review*, and it's easy to see how *assessment* underlies and complements *revision*. When the writer goes back to the text to take another look, what the writer sees *in the text itself* is the review or *assessment* part of the process. What the writer sees *in his or her mind*—the new vision, the new connections—is the *revision*. Revisioning, or revising, the text gives the writer a way of sharing new insights: The writer reshapes and reorders the text to make it match, as nearly as possible, the new vision in his or her head. Reviewing, or assessing, the text allows the writer to see where his or her thinking has been and to use his or her own words to make new connections.

ASSESSMENT: THE TRADITIONAL VIEW

. . . even though there are many good ways to think and write, it seems clear that excellence must involve finding *some* way to be both abundantly inventive yet toughmindedly critical (Elbow, 1987, 171).

If we consider the relationship between the writing process and the traditional view of assessment, we notice three things. First, most traditional models of the writing process tend to start with "prewriting" and to end with evaluation or assessment, or to leave this step out altogether. Omitting assessment from the cycle leaves student writers and teachers dangling. Assessment, even if it's only in the form of self-evaluation and nothing more, gives writers and teachers a sense of closing the circle.

Second, assessment (in most traditional writing models, process-oriented or not) tends to be teacher-directed. It's the teacher who is entrusted with the job of making judgments about the quality of the writing produced.

Third, assessment tends to be associated with grades. This isn't always the case, but it tends to be the case. The problem is that these three elements—(1) placing assessment at the end of the writing process; (2) allowing assessment to be strictly teacher-oriented; and (3) automatically equating assessment with grading or some other form of final judgment—all tend to weaken the potential of assessment for helping students improve their writing. What should we do about this? First, we should make assessment an integral part of the writing process and not an afterthought. Second, we should teach students to assess their own writing, so that teachers and student writers share assessment responsibility and learn from assessment results. Third, we ensure that assessment results serve the *full range* of purposes in the classroom, from diagnosing students' needs, to grouping students for instruction, to evaluating this instruction, and, finally, to evaluating students' performance. We ensure that some assessment, in the form of interim feedback, occurs prior to or apart from grading (or both), so that students learn to write for the joy and the satisfaction of writing.

Getting Ready to Assess

In deciding what to assess, you might begin by asking your students what they value in good writing. Think about what you value as a reader. Together you can create a list of traits that you'll assess when you finish drafting and get ready to assess. Your list might look something like this one:

_____ Ideas		_____ Fluency	
_____ Support		_____ Spelling	
_____ Word choice and phrasing		_____ Mechanics	
_____ Voice			

Remember, this is just a sample list; it doesn't have to look like yours. Whatever list you come up with, however, keep in mind that the writer is often the best judge of *when* to assess; the writer knows when he or she is ready to accept and to use the responses of others and when they're just getting in the way. From the student's perspective, the best time to assess might be after the first draft, the second, or the fifth. From the teacher's perspective, there are four strategically ideal ways to work assessment into the writing process: through comments, peer review, conferencing, and revision.

INTERVENTION THAT WORKS

Intervention sounds like something that gets in the way. This is the trouble with jargon—it always sounds like something else. What we mean, of course, by *intervention* is not getting in the writer's way but moving in at just the right moment with just the right kind of support. This is effective intervention, especially when it's enhanced with a sound approach to assessment that empowers student writers.

The Saga of Smith and Jones

In order to better appreciate the importance of good intervention, consider the instructional approaches of two teachers: Smith and Jones. Smith takes a rather rigorous approach to writing assessment. He suffers from a mounting fear that increasing numbers of students will slip through the cracks without learning to write and that part of the blame for this disgrace will be his. He means to do what he can. He gives weekly assignments for which all students are responsible. They dread these assignments, and so does he.

All writing is done outside of the class. Papers cannot be late. If a student is absent, some trusted messenger must deliver the paper to Smith's class on time. Every paper has a minimum number of words, which varies from 250 to 1,000.

Smith doesn't believe in giving hints about how to approach a given topic. He tells students bluntly that it is up to them to figure out what is required and that this is part of learning to write. In fact, reading Smith's mind is the key to getting top grades in his class.

Smith's style is squeaky clean of intervention prior to grading. His students do not brainstorm ideas or interview one another, and he does not offer any suggestions on how student writers can enrich their experiential base. His student writers do not write or revise their papers in class, nor do they share their writing or ideas with one another in support groups. He holds no conferences. Grades may or may not be accompanied by comments (usually negative), but, in any case, by the time the student receives the comment, Smith has made sure that it's too late to do anything about it.

Jones also feels the relentless tides of ignorance sweeping through her frail fingers, but her way of handling the situation is quite different from Smith's. In fact, she finds Smith's approach appalling, though she would not tell him so to his face. She could never be like him. Her mission is to help. She feels a personal responsibility to make sure everybody's writing gets fixed. She accomplishes this by scanning everything her student writers produce. She doesn't *read* everything, but she does *proofread* it—all of it. Jones's students don't have to wonder where the spelling mistakes are or which punctuation marks are faulty; she circles them. Her students' margins spill over with

Teachers who habitually try to mark every error in a paper, no matter what the cost to themselves, may wind up unintentionally giving their students two very negative messages: first, that they really do not care what students say, they only care that they say it correctly; and second, that they consider teaching writing a great burden and a thankless task (Hairston, 1986, 121).

exhortations to be specific, start new paragraphs, stop generalizing. This work is exhausting, and though Jones doesn't like to admit it even to herself, she deeply resents her students' obvious lack of appreciation.

Jones's approach may be different from Smith's, but she isn't using intervention effectively; in fact, she's doing all the work herself. Her students don't have to take responsibility for their own writing: She edits; they fill in the blanks. This way, there's less risk of error. Are her students writing better? That's hard to say. But Jones's proofreading skills are beyond reproach.

Jones and Smith are real characters, of course. Maybe you know them. I've met Jones quite a few times, in and out of school. My version of her is a little on the wimpy side, I admit. The real Jones has considerably more backbone than her fictionalized counterpart, but she's overburdened with her sense of responsibility, and it's draining valuable energy from her.

I met Smith only once. He was a teacher of mine, long ago and far away, and I probably learned more from him than I care to admit, but most of it was by default. He was a teacher of literature first and foremost, and he pursued it like a calling. To him, the teaching of composition was an interference, an intrusion, a bother. He enjoyed handing out assignments only marginally more than the class enjoyed responding to them.

We learned to see Smith's assignments for what they were: traps, snares for the weak, the unimaginative, the wasters of time. He didn't like our lack of sensitivity to syntax and meant to make us pay. He was also offended (not mildly offended—incensed) by our blatant disregard for proper spelling or the conventions of punctuation. At the time, it never occurred to us that he didn't have every right in the world to feel this way. Anyone who wrote as badly as we did, we reasoned, probably deserved to be intimidated by difficult assignments and humiliated by harsh marginal comments. Only now, so many years later, do I realize how very much some of us probably had to say and how very much Smith missed.

What might Smith and Jones have done differently? For one thing, both might have written with their students. This would have enabled them to focus less on perfecting the product—the piece of writing— and more on helping the students use the process of writing to learn. Both might also have used assessment more creatively, not just to grade or to correct copy but to provide real responses to students' writing and to offer feedback at the time when it's most useful—when the writing is still in process.

There are four critical ways in which teachers can intervene or step in *very* effectively. Each of these bears some relationship to how and why writing assessment in the classroom is conducted. These are through (1) positive comments, (2) peer response groups, (3) conferencing, and (4) revision.

INTERVENTION 1: POSITIVE COMMENTS

We've already emphasized the importance of being interested and responsive readers, but this doesn't mean that we have to be editorial slaves. Anyone who's ever worked as an editor will tell you that lazy writers like nothing better than the comfort of knowing that "the editor will fix it." Not only will the conscientious editor patch up problems with syntax, punctuation, and spelling, but she or he will agonize over hidden meanings and struggle to create form out of chaos. This is why editors get cranky. They have a right. A cranky disposition, however, doesn't lend itself to inspiration in the classroom. The moral is, if you're teaching composition, don't make yourself an editor for 150 people every week. Both you and they will resent it. Furthermore, although you'll learn a great deal about editing and proofreading, those for whom you edit will only learn to depend on you.

How to Respond to Students' Writing

Here's a chance to find out how to respond to students' writing. Look at the following student paper. It's an eighth-grader's discussion of friendship. Skim through it. Ask yourself how many marks you'd need to make on this paper if you identified all the errors. What grade would you give it? What comment(s) would you make to the student? Write these down, in the book or on a piece of scratch paper.

ERNIE, MY BEST FRIEND

Ernie is a fun person to be with, at least for me, and I cannot begin to recight all we did together. However I could give a few examples. For example, we used to swim in an old stone quarry over by his house. There was a tower in the pond that he used to haul himself up to the top of. Then I'd toss him a steel cable attached to a beam. He would then hurl himself into the deep green murk and disapear whith a splash. And what a splash! Once he swam the whole four hundred and twenty meters of the pond. He didn't even stop to pant.

We also went on skating parties together. He's the one who tried to teach me how to skate. I still don't know despite his efforts.

When we whern't swimming or skating we might have been playing Role Playing Games, our favorite pastime. It was not particularily mine though. He liked to play Gamma World, I liked Star Frontiers.

Ernie had a lot friends here despite his rather unsighly round stature. But when he moved to Ithaca he had trouble making friends. That was the biggest surprise of my life.

I suppose you need to know what Ernie looks like. Well his not the most beutifull frined in the world. he had a kind of amber colored eye. they were wide and kind eyes. Made you want to like him. he had a sort of blonde mix whith brown hair. That hair was always clean and striaght and stayed close to his head. he also a very tight color of skin that fit nicely around his bulbous bod. I suppose thats why he had trouble making friends down there because he was so large.

But he was my best friend, and always will be.

GRADE _____

COMMENTS:

What amount of time did you spend? *How* did you spend it? What comments did you make to the writer? It's fairly easy to put yourself in the role of the teacher; most of us are used to this by now. Imagine for a moment, though, that you are the student writer of the preceding paper. You have received the comments you wrote. How do you feel about them? Keep your comments in mind; we'll return to them in a moment.

Obviously, editing and proofreading are time consuming. What's the alternative? The alternative is to focus on the message, to respond to the content and to the voice, to think positively, and look for what's right and point it out, in specific terms. Deal with problems, pitfalls, and errors in another way, another time.

If you are using an analytical scoring scale to respond to students' writing, you'll have comments built in by the way your criteria are defined, but if you are not using an analytical scoring scale, then as you read a student's paper, ask yourself the same sorts of questions that you'd ask if you were assessing it analytically. Is the theme coming through? Does it begin effectively? Does it wrap up well? How's the pacing? Does it move you along? Which characters are most interesting? Which descriptions hold your attention? Which comments are most persuasive? Is the voice appealing, powerful? Find a phrase, an image, an insightful remark or a transition that catches your eye. (There's always *something*.) Underline it. Underline up to three or four words, passages, phrases, or sections that catch or hold your attention. Then write one positive comment at the end of the paper.

Take another look at the paper on Ernie. This time, just underline one or more passages *that strike you*. Then, write *one positive comment* at the end of the paper.

COMMENTS AFTER SECOND READING:

How much time did you spend with the paper this time through? Did your comment(s) to the student change at all? Again, put yourself in the student's place. How did you respond?

Here, by the way, are the phrases that most teachers have noted as striking in this paper:

". . . hurl himself into the deep green murk . . ."
"And what a splash!"
"He didn't even stop to pant."
". . . despite his efforts."
". . . his rather unsighly round stature."
". . . a kind of amber colored eye."
". . . stayed close to his head."
". . . fit nicely around his bulbous bod."

When you underscore what strikes you in a paper, you say to the writer, "I noticed this. It stood out." For the writer who is writing to be read, no response can be more satisfying.

Positive and Negative Comments

As teachers, we may sometimes get the feeling that no one is paying attention to us, that no one is responding to our efforts. In fact, student writers usually *are* responding to our comments but sometimes not in the way we think.

Here are some examples of students' responses to negative comments on their papers. They're taken from an arbitrary, nonrepresentative sampling of high-school students in a suburban school district who were told to be completely honest and that their responses would be anonymous. Do any of these comments or the responses to them seem familiar?

STUDENTS' RESPONSES TO TEACHERS' COMMENTS

When the teacher wrote:

Needs work.

Students reacted this way:

Too general. I wouldn't learn anything from this comment.
Kind of rude. Work on what?
I feel cheap.
I'm discouraged.
Pretty harsh.
Makes me feel hopeless.
Failed; defeated.
I would ignore it because it makes me hate the teacher.

When the teacher wrote:

Concentrate more on mechanics.

Students reacted this way:

This makes me mad!

I have no idea what this means.
I wish the teacher would write so I could understand.
Inadequate; confused.
Usually, I use my most recent learned words that are big for me so it is
a put down.
Learn punctuation—"You're stupid."
My grammar is bad and creativity means nothing.

When the teacher wrote:

Use examples to show what you mean.

Students reacted this way:

Why? If I give examples on every detail I'll never get the point of my
whole paper across!
Boring.
OK, like what?
Frustration, because I've worked on it a lot and done the best I could.

When the teacher wrote:

Needs to be more concise.

Students reacted this way:

Confusing. I need to know what the teacher means specifically.
This is an obvious comment.
I'm not Einstein. I can't get every point right.
I muffed.
I thought you wanted details and support.
This frustrates me!
Define "concise."
Vague, vague.

Children, like adults, learn best in a supportive context. They are more apt to remember kind words about their successes than harsh words about their failures (Calkins, 1986, 209).

When the teacher wrote:

Be more specific.

Students reacted this way:

You be specific.
I'm frustrated.
I tried and it didn't pay off.
It's going to be too long then.
I feel mad—it really doesn't matter.
I try, but I don't know every fact.

When the teacher wrote:

Stronger verbs.

Students reacted this way:

What do you think I am? I lack verby power.
Should have used a thesaurus.

This is confusing.
So what!? I thought they were fine.
My vocab is bad.
I don't know any other verbs.
Confused. I'll write the way I choose to.
My choice, not yours.
I feel dumb.

When the teacher wrote:

Weak ending.

Students reacted this way:

I have trouble writing endings. Teachers are no help!
Weak? No way—that's a great ending!
Then help me.
I feel bad. *You* need a better conclusion.
Defeated. What do you suggest?

When the teacher wrote:

Not up to your usual efforts.

Students reacted this way:

This is depressing.
That's opinionated.
I'm going through bad times in my life—not up to writing a paper.
Maybe I found this assignment hard.
This makes me mad!
Something to be said by maybe one's mother.
I don't learn anything from this on how to better the paper.

When the teacher wrote:

You haven't really thought this through.

Students reacted this way:

That is a mean reply.
I guess I blew it!
I'm upset.
That makes me madder than you can imagine!
How do you know what I thought?

When the teacher wrote:

Try harder!

Students reacted this way:

I did try!
You're a stupid jerk.
Maybe I am trying as hard as I can.
I feel like kicking the teacher.
Baloney! You don't know how hard I tried.

This kind of comment makes me feel really bad and I'm frustrated!
All right, all right.
If we turned it in, it means we tried.

As you can see (and as you already know instinctively), negative comments, however well intentioned they are, tend to make students feel bewildered, hurt, or angry. They stifle further attempts at writing. It would seem on the face of it that one good way to help a budding writer would be to point out what he or she is doing wrong, but, in fact, it usually doesn't help; it hurts. Sometimes it hurts a lot.

What does help, however, is to point out what the writer is doing well. Positive comments build confidence and make the writer want to try again. However, there's a trick to writing *good* positive comments. They must be truthful, and they must be *very* specific. It's one thing to say, "Good job, John." This is not negative, but it's very general. You should know that it can, and often does, sound phoney. Think of a four-year-old who is showing off his new bike-riding skills to a father who's engrossed in the stock market report. "Look at me, Dad! Look at me!" the four-year-old shouts, over and over. Dad maintains a running commentary—"Great, son, just great"—without ever looking up. No one appreciates this mindless kind of approval. You must show by your comments that you have read the paper, and you've got to mean what you say: "I liked the part where you set the eagle free—and I could tell that was hard for you." Now you're showing that you were paying attention.

Sometimes it's tough. Maybe you really don't like the paper, or there just isn't much there. Don't give up. Look again. Look for a single word that strikes a responsive chord. Underline it. If you can't find even one, then keep your task simple: Look for capitalization used correctly, a tricky word spelled right, a centered title, quotation marks well placed. Start as small as you must. (See Figure 4.2.).

Figure 4.3 is another example of an eighth-grade paper on friendship as one teacher marked it, with the errors circled. Imagine yourself receiving this paper. How would you respond? Now here is an equally important question: Does this kind of error hunting accomplish anything beneficial? Research overwhelmingly indicates that it does not (Hillocks, 1986). Studies cited by Maxine Hairston (1986) suggest that students find negative comments and corrections bewildering, confusing, offensive, intimidating, and generally useless. Overwhelmed by the impossibility of it all, students either shrug and give up or adapt a defensive, defiant stance, showing their contempt for what their English teachers regard as so important.

Nevertheless, many of us still see in our heads the old models, the wielders of red pens who corrected and harangued us. Do we just ignore the errors? No. We need the courage, however, to admit that the old ways of "teaching" conventions did not work. We will have to find others.

Correction merely highlights what learners almost certainly know they cannot do in the first place. Correction is worthwhile only if the learner would seek it in any case, and to seek correction for what you do, you must regard yourself as a professional. . . . Emphasis on the elimination of mistakes results in the elimination of writing (Smith, 1984, 56).

Teachers who assign only the amount of writing that they can "mark" thoroughly are doing a great disservice to their students. It has been said many times before, but I will repeat it: all papers need not be analyzed for every error; all papers need not be graded (Tate, 1981, 68).

NEG	POS	POS-SPEC
Try harder!	Good job!	I couldn't stop laughing about that dog eating the marshmallow
Work on the spelling.	I see some improvement here — B+	You knew that "a lot" was two words — good for you!
Did you proofread this!?!	Nice try.	You spelled "Cincinnati" right — that's not an easy one.
Parts of this just don't make sense — re-read!	Great organization!	Your opening sentence got me hooked right away.

FIGURE 4.2. Brainstorming

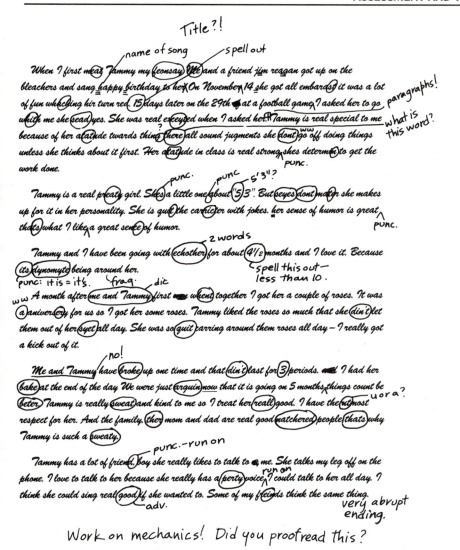

FIGURE 4.3. Eighth-Grade Paper

What Terrible Things Will Happen to Me If I Abandon the Red Pen?

Let's face it, nothing is ever easy. If you give up marking papers with red pens, the following troubles are likely to haunt you. First, some colleagues will disapprove. Expect shock, resentment, and some overt criticism. You will appear to some people to be shirking your rightful responsibility as a teacher. Which brings us to another problem.

Some parents also will disapprove. "What are you teaching our kids," they will want to know, "if you are not teaching them to spell and

When I examine whole files of papers that have been marked and commented on by teachers, many of them look as though they have been trampled on by cleated boots (Diederich, 1974, 20).

to punctuate?'' Notice that this question entails an assumption so big, so large, and so looming, that only a few people have thought to question its validity. The assumption is that correcting errors is somehow related to the teaching of such things as spelling and punctuation. Never mind that there's no real evidence that this is so. Old superstitions die hard. The truth is, students *can* learn editing skills through the circling and fixing of errors *if* (and only if) they are doing the circling and fixing.

Finally, you may feel guilty if you've been used to proofreading what your students write. You may feel that suddenly things have gotten too easy or that you're being too soft on yourself. Those red marks are real and tangible and make you feel as if you're doing something. (You are.) Before, you could thumb through that stack of 150 papers when you were done and have the satisfaction of knowing that another 15,000 errors had bitten the dust. Now, here you are, abdicating the considerable power that goes with being an editor-in-charge, turning the job over to someone else—who probably won't do it as well. You may be haunted by the fear that in the name of innovation you've abandoned your concern for good writing. You haven't, of course, but plenty of people will be delighted to tell you otherwise, and you may find it hard not to listen.

> Research suggests that the finer points of writing, such as punctuation and subject-verb agreement, are learned best while students are engaged in extended writing that has the purpose of communicating a message to an audience (Anderson et al., 1985, 80).

What Good Things Will Happen to Me If I Give Up Hunting for Errors?

If you give up hunting for errors, first, you'll have more time to actually teach writing. You'll still be *reading* what students write, but you'll find it goes faster when you aren't *proofreading* it.

Second, you'll begin to concentrate more on what they have to say. It's hard to think about the opera if your shoes are too tight, and it's hard to focus on the message if you're hunting for errors. Now you can be free of all this. Kick those tight shoes off, lean back, and allow yourself to read your students' writing the way you read other literature. (Ah, that feels better.)

Third, and best of all, you'll find that most students will not feel so intimidated about writing. They'll begin to enjoy it. They'll actually start to believe you when you say that you care about the message more than about the grammar and the spelling. They'll want to write more because it's satisfying to play to an appreciative audience (and never to one that isn't). They'll *want* to fix the conventions because they won't want you—the appreciative audience—to miss anything.

Then comes the very best surprise of all: Students' writing will improve. Yes, it will. *It will get better faster once you stop marking all the errors.* How can this be? There are two reasons: First, you will no longer be stifling incentive and motivation through overt criticism. Students who do not care whether their writing gets read have little reason to care about making it readable. Second, you will find other, more

> There seems to be little value in marking students' papers with ''corrections,'' little value in teaching the conventions of mechanics apart from actual writing, and even less value in teaching grammar in order to instill these conventions (Weaver, 1979, 64).

effective ways of teaching sentence structure, grammar, and conventions.

Here's one suggestion. If you feel you *must* respond to the conventions in a student's paper, you can mark what is done correctly, as shown in Figure 4.4.

Here are some other suggestions for teaching conventions effectively:

Somehow we lost sight of the teaching precept: What you make a child love and desire is more important than what you make him learn (Trelease, 1985, 6).

1. Ask students to mark their own papers.
2. Ask students to share with you, in conference, the reasons behind

good try - I knew what you meant.

good transition here

When I first meat Tammy my feonsay Me and a friend jim reagan got up on the bleachers and sang happy birthday to her On November 14 she got all embarast it was a lot of fun whaching hir turn red. 15 days later on the 29th at a football game I asked her to go whith me she sead yes. She was real exceyted when I asked her. Tammy is real special to me because of her atatude twards thing there all sound jugments she dont go off doing things unless she thinks about it first. Her atatude in class is real strong shes determin to get the work done.

good - it is one word

good! spelled right!

good

almost

good place to begin a new ¶

Tammy is a real preaty girl. Shes a little one about "5 3". But seyes dont mater she makes up for it in her personality. She is quit the carricter with jokes. her sense of humor is great thats what I like a great sence of humor

excellent

or, yes - good

Tammy and I have been going with echother for about 41/2 months and I love it. Because its dynomyte being around her.

this fragment works well - sounds very natural.

A month after me and Tammy first when whent together I got her a couple of roses. It was a aniversery for us so I got her some roses. Tammy liked the roses so much that she din't let them out of her syet all day. She was so quit carring around them roses all day — I really got a kick out of it.

all periods here in the right places - ends of sentences - great!

good variety here in sentence length - some longer, some shorter.

Me and Tammy have broke up one time and that din't last for 3 periods. and I had her bake at the end of the day We were just arguin now that it is going on 5 months things count be beter. Tammy is really sweat and kind to me so I treat her reall good. I have the atmost respect for her. And the family. ther mom and dad are real good natchered people thats why Tammy is such a sweaty.

almost right - is that a "u"? utmost is right

you knew "a lot" was two words - good for you.

Tammy has a lot of friend. boy she really likes to talk to to me. She talks my leg off on the phone. I love to talk to her because she really has a perty voice I could talk to her all day. I think she could sing real good if she wanted to. Some of my freinds think the same thing.

I feel I know Tammy, too. Your warm feelings come through. Thanks for sharing.

good use of capitals at beginnings of sentences.

FIGURE 4.4. Marking What Is Done Correctly

In both reading and writing, errors have meaning. . . . Work in spelling research suggests that mistakes made by young writers may not be mistakes at all, but rather, can be considered part of the children's growth pattern as writers (Chew, 1985, 172).

We should see our students as smart and capable. We should assume that they *can* learn what we teach—all of them. We should look *through* their mistakes or ignorance to the intelligence that lies behind (Elbow, 1987, 149).

their "errors." Remember, there's often a logic to what students do, even if it differs from your logic. You have a better chance of changing any behavior if you know the reason behind it.

3. Ask students to edit in groups where each benefits from the others' expertise.

4. Focus on *one* kind of error only, say, capitalization at the beginning of sentences.

5. Keep records of what students *can* do. Let them help. They can keep cards on which they list their editorial accomplishments.

6. Teach proofreaders' marks to simplify the editing process for students. (See Figure 4.5.)

Marvin ~~believe it or not~~ is here.	Delete.
Marvin i s here.	Close up; delete space.
Mar͜vin is here.	Delete and close up.
Marvin‌is here.	Insert space.
Marvin‌is here.	Separate words.
Marvin ‸ here.	Insert a word or phrase.
¶	Begin a new paragraph.
No ¶	No new paragraph. Run paragraphs together.
Marvin is here⊙	Insert a period.
Is Marvin here⸝?⸝	Insert a question mark.
Marvin, who is hardly ever on time‸is finally here.	Insert a comma.
Marvin is here‸so is Fred.	Insert a semicolon.
Here's the surprise of the century‸Marvin is here.	Insert a colon.
̲marvin is here.	Capitalize.
Marvin is /Here.	Use lower case.
Marvin brought his ③ fish. ᔆᵖ	Spell this word out.
Marvin's fish are here.	Insert an apostrophe.
Marvin said, ˮHere are my fish˶	Insert quotation marks.
Marvin ⸜here⁄is⸝	Transpose words.
Ma⸜rv⁄in is h⸜er⁄e.	Transpose letters.

FIGURE 4.5. Proofreaders' Marks

7. Teach students to score student writing analytically for the trait of conventions and then to back up their scores with a discussion of the strengths and weaknesses that they find in the papers.

8. Mechanics: Giv thm some unedted copie lik this thet let's their sea what happens? When, convintions is use incorrect. Porlie written copey helpsthem seee the valeu; of Strong conventions in Klewing. The reader?

9. Ask students to look for other examples of text (from books, newspapers, letters, ads) in which conventions are well used or poorly used. Score the samples on the trait of conventions and discuss the relationship between the scores and the readability of the text.

"Be careful what you say, . . ." Comments stick with us sometimes for years. Stop and think of your own situation. Can you recall, as a student writer, receiving a negative comment that really hurt? Can you recall a positive comment that really encouraged you? Here are a few of both that other teachers have recalled. As you read them, keep in mind that in many classrooms comments (oral or written) are the most prevalent form of assessment.

TEACHERS RECALL THE GOOD TIMES . . .

Good clear thinking—you always develop your ideas completely and show good insight about the reading.

Appears to be from personal experience—very moving and conveys emotions to the reader.

You have a special way with words!

You have a creative soul!

You have a great touch—a great way to express your feelings.

You have a real gift.

It is clear to me you intend to be a great teacher, and I would say you are well on your way.

I like the way you wrote this sentence. It makes me feel as if I am right there with you.

I like the way you write. You say what you have to say, then quit. This sounds as if it really happened.

I want to read more. Beautiful. Love it!

Continue with this—I'd like to read more!

This is the way to use supporting details!

Nice try! I've often thought about that myself.

Beautiful sentence rhythm.

You told me you couldn't write. You *can.* This proves it.

Thank you for sharing your poem. It spoke to me.

The way words move through you, through your pen—I envy that, love that.

. . . AND THE NOT SO GOOD TIMES

I can't believe what I see here. There is *nothing* of worth, except that the documentation is perfect. It is only the documentation that boosts this paper to a D-.

Ugh!

I think you may have it in you to write competently but not brilliantly.

In looking at this paper again, I believe it is even worse than I originally thought.

You don't know how to write.

Do you really understand the word "proletariat"?

Be more concise! Not so many commas!

Your most irritating habit is your persistent, relentless misuse of the semicolon.

You'll never be an author.

What in the *world* are you trying to say!?! Just spit it out.

Do over!!

This does not make sense.

See me!

No! This isn't your work.

Your writing reminds me of a porcupine—many points leading in meaningless directions.

Prove it.

You missed the point completely. F.

This couldn't possibly be your best effort.

Dialogue doesn't work—sounds stilted, phoney. *No one* talks this way.

No, I don't think so—I just don't think so.

Remember: One person's marginal whimsy is another's lifetime memory. Think before you write.

INTERVENTION 2: PEER REVIEW

As we've seen, when assessment focuses on strengths, not just on tracking down errors, it enables teachers to make the kinds of positive comments that build confidence and motivate students to write. Let's look now at a second kind of intervention, one that can also make good use of assessment but in a slightly different way.

■ SCENARIO

Ruth and Frank are having lunch. "Give me some tips on peer review," Ruth says, "and I'll tell you Hamlet's three tragic flaws."

"I already know Hamlet's three tragic flaws," Frank retorts, "and one of them was putting too much faith in peer review."

"Come on," Ruth chides, "what's wrong with peer review?"

"It doesn't work, that's what. It's the blind leading the blind. Listen. You've got a bunch of kids trying to learn to write, right? You stick them in groups, and one is supposed to teach the other. Give me a break. They don't listen. If they *do* comment, half the time it's something either meaningless like, "Really good, Harold" or else it's something tactless that ruins poor Harold's day. Besides this, they don't know what they're talking about. They don't know enough about writing to teach it. You know what happens in those groups? They talk about the Friday football game or who's got a date, and nothing to do with writing. I'm telling you, peer review is a waste of time."   ■

Peer review *can* be a waste of time if it's little more than a social hour. It doesn't have to be like that. It's disheartening to hear a teacher say, "Peer review? Oh, I tried that once. It didn't work." Peer review is a little like the back flip: You can't just try it once. When it doesn't succeed, it's usually for one of the following reasons:

1. The teacher doesn't believe entirely in the process or doesn't model the process for students in a way that lets them see the power of having an audience, or both.
2. The students lack a working vocabulary with which to talk about writing.
3. The students have a hard time listening and have had little opportunity to build listening skills.
4. The students equate criticism with failure and feel intimidated by any comments, however tactfully they are structured.
5. The students have a hard time drawing the line between tactful and bland. Resulting comments are sometimes so general that the writer can make nothing of them. Moreover, the group sessions are so dull that no one wants to meet again.
6. The students simply do not know what to do, and they wind up rushing through all the papers, huddling in uncomfortable silence, chatting about other things, or staring out the window.

The following are some suggestions to help teachers make peer review more successful:

1. Participate. Don't just explain *how;* do it. Share your own writing with the class, let them practice summarizing what they've heard, noting whatever struck them most, asking questions. Model the kind of response that you'd like to see the students give. Show them how to take it in, sift it, and let responders know when *you* (as the writer) need clarification or when you've had enough.

2. Model some good and bad peer-review groups in front of the class. Get student volunteers to help you demonstrate the kind of behavior that works (good listening skills, positive comments, specific comments, insightful questions), and the kind that does not (not listening, being negative, looking bored, having nothing to say, telling the writer what to do). Let others in the class comment on what works and what doesn't.

3. Videotape or audiotape some sessions and play them back for the class. Audiotaping is particularly effective when you cannot be everywhere at once but would like to give groups a way of sharing how or why their process worked or didn't work.

4. Teach students to assess writing analytically. In doing so, you'll help them develop

> a critic's perspective
> a working vocabulary with which to talk about writing
> an understanding that writing—*all* writing—is a mixture of strengths and weaknesses
> an ability, drawing on their new working vocabulary, to make specific, useful comments to peers: for example, "Your introduction worked very well"; "Your paper ended at just the right spot"; "The voice was especially strong on this first page—it really sounded like you."

Some teachers argue for the value of simple emotional responses to a piece of writing. There's nothing wrong with this. It's fine for students to say things like, "That piece just gave me chills" or "I couldn't wait to find out what happened to Aunt Effie's hat." Any comment that reveals the reader's (or, in this case, the listener's) genuine response to the writing has value. In *Embracing Contraries,* Peter Elbow (1987) makes a convincing case for playing "movies of the mind" or telling the story of one's personal response to the writer's text. Elbow is right. This kind of feedback *is* powerful, but there is also some value, especially for the student writer who is wondering how to revise a piece, in knowing whether the voice is powerful and appealing, whether the ideas are clear and focused, and whether the organization is well developed.

5. Read samples of students' writing and your own writing to the class as a whole. Get students used to hearing papers read aloud. They play differently to the ear than to the eye. Hearing the organization or the voice within the paper takes time. Be patient. The listening skills will come.

6. Read literature aloud often. Give students a chance to *hear* it, not just see it. Let them read aloud too so that each text plays in many voices. Encourage students to respond to a piece of literature *as writing*. In other words, although it's fine to discuss plot, theme, and characterization, it's also vital to talk about how each writer achieves these things. Does the introduction pull you in? If so, why? Do the characters seem real? Why? Responding orally *and* in writing to many texts builds assessment skills, and when assessment skills are strong, peer review feels more natural and less contrived.

What Really Goes on in Peer Groups

Just tossing students together and hoping for the magic to happen doesn't work very well. Students want and need some structure, at least at first.

Here's one model for a peer review—a compilation of the best suggestions that we've gathered from teachers during the past several years:

1. Students gather in groups of three or four (no more or it will take too long to read and to respond to all the papers properly). In some classes, pairs work well, especially if students are fearful about reading aloud, even in very small groups.

2. One by one, each writer within a given group reads his. or her piece aloud while others listen.

3. Before any discussion, the writer may read the paper a second time so that listeners can get any details that they missed or make notes. Often the writer will take a deep breath, slow down, and give the text a more fair reading the second time.

4. Each listener *briefly* sums up the piece as he or she hears it. This allows the writer to discover whether listeners are making the same connections he made as a writer and whether the text offers new meanings that should be clarified or extended. Listeners may also, at this point, give their personal responses to the text, not just "I heard . . ." but also "I felt . . ." and "I thought. . . ." It is very helpful for writers to know not only whether the message as content is getting through but also how it's affecting the readers or listeners.

5. Each listener (based on notes or memory) identifies words, phrases, or images that particularly stand out. (This is the oral

version of what you do when you underline bits of text that "stick in your mind.") The listener does not have to say "I really *liked* the part where...." Whatever is striking or impressive enough to recall is the key here.

6. Every listener *may*, but does not have to, ask a question about something that was unclear or something that the listener would like to know more about.

7. The writer *may*, but does not have to, ask for suggestions or responses to specific sections or writing approaches.

8. Listeners do not make negative comments (e.g., "I just didn't like it") and do not tell the writer directly what to do (e.g., "Get rid of the first paragraph"), but they may respond to direct questions from the writer (e.g., "Do you think it would work better if I hacked off the first paragraph?").

9. At least occasionally, one person within each group acts as a recorder and makes notes of comments and questions that seem to work well or to cause problems.

10. During a short debriefing session at the end of the class, students talk about the writing and about the peer-review process itself, offering criticisms or suggesting improvements.

Students need to understand that responding to a piece isn't the same as taking responsiblity for fixing it. The writer—and only the writer—has the right and the responsibility to make revisions.

Here is another effective model for students who are familiar with analytical scoring. Students should use this model with anonymous papers, *not their own*. (Having their own papers scored analytically by peers is too threatening for most students.)

1. Students break into groups of three or four.

2. Within each small group, students circulate papers until each student has read and scored all the papers. Students may score papers on just one trait (e.g., voice) or on more than one trait, depending on the teacher's objectives and the students' scoring skill. Scores are marked on scratch paper, not on the papers themselves.

3. Once all scoring is completed, each writer reads one of the papers aloud.

4. Students then share and compare scores on one or more traits, explaining the reasons behind their scores, listening to the responses of others, and discussing the variations in response to the same text. Each listener or reader identifies what he or she feels to be *the strongest* trait of each paper.

An important advantage to this approach is that it requires students to respond to a piece of writing individually and independently *before* they have an opportunity to be influenced by what others think and feel.

Students who use analytical scoring as part of the peer review can use a scoring guide like the one given in Chapter 2, or they can use a checklist like the one following (a similar but differently structured checklist appears in Chapter 7):

GUIDE TO REVISION

Ideas and Content

( ) My paper has a clear purpose or makes a point.

( ) I use clear, relevant details and examples to help the reader understand my message.

( ) I stick to the main idea (or ideas) and leave out details that do not matter.

( ) I have thought about my topic carefully and feel as if I know what I'm talking about.

Organization

( ) The way I've started my paper is effective; it would make the reader want to keep reading.

( ) I've told things in an order that makes sense and makes it easy to follow what I'm saying.

( ) The details in my paper go together or lead up to some bigger idea, main point, or conclusion.

( ) My paper ends well; it doesn't just stop suddenly, but it doesn't drag on too long either.

Voice

( ) I've written in a way that shows how *I* really think and feel about this topic.

( ) I like what I've written; it's fun to read.

( ) I've put something of myself into this paper and it sounds like me—not like someone else.

( ) I've given some thought to what the reader will think and feel while reading this.

Word Choice

( ) It's easy to picture what I'm talking about; the words paint a picture in the reader's mind.

( ) I wasn't satisfied with words or phrases I've heard many times before; I've tried to find my own way to say things.

( ) My writing sounds natural; it sounds like me.

( ) Sometimes I've tried saying something in a new or a different way; I've had fun with the language.

Sentence Fluency

( ) My sentences make sense; the meaning of each one is clear, and there are no words left out.

( ) My sentences have variety; some are longer than others, and they do not all begin the same way.

( ) I've read my paper over and I like the way it sounds; it's smooth and easy to read.

Conventions

( ) I've proofread my paper and corrected any errors in spelling, punctuation, or grammar.

( ) My paragraphs begin in the right spots.

( ) I've used capital letters to begin sentences and on all proper nouns (*names* of persons, places, or things).

( ) Correct spelling, punctuation, grammar, capitalization, and paragraphing would make this paper easy for anyone to pick up and read out loud.

When to Meet

Human beings have a deep need to represent their experience through writing. We need to make our truths beautiful (Calkins, 1986, 3).

Most people who use peer review wedge it in somewhere between drafting and revision, and sometimes as a preamble to revision. This is logical, and if there isn't time for groups to meet more than once, this is probably the best time to meet.

On the other hand, consider that professional writers, given an opportunity to work with a colleague, generally collaborate long before drafting. Think about the value, then, of peer-*support* groups—groups that would meet for the first time as a part of prewriting. These groups would tackle an assignment as a problem-solving task: "What's the purpose of this writing?" "Who's our audience?" "How shall we go about it?" Later, when they meet again to review one another's drafts, they'd have some context for that review, and they could ask more relevant and useful questions; "Did we fulfill the purpose we said was important?" "Did we think about the needs of our audience?" "Was our approach effective?"

■ SCENARIO

Lois is in her third year of teaching eighth-grade English. She's been placing more emphasis on composition in the last two years, but this is the first time that she's tried peer review in her class, and she isn't at all sure that she or her students will like it. She is following the suggestions of a consultant from a workshop on the writing process and is planning to demonstrate peer review in front of the class. She has arranged the chairs in a big circle, where everyone can see her and be heard. The total class, Lois explains, is larger than the peer groups will be. For practice, however, and for purposes of modeling the process, she wants to give everyone a chance to participate.

She reads her paper aloud and feels a lot more nervous than she thought she would. It's a paper about "a favorite object"—her car. As she reads, she silently berates herself for not spending more time on the paper. She doesn't like the sound of it. The introduction drones on forever. It's corny, she thinks. She wonders vaguely why she chose to write about her car in the first place. It isn't her "favorite object." The car doesn't even run very well. She chose it because it seemed easy to describe.

She feels tense. She isn't used to reading her work out loud in front of the class and wonders how they will like being instructed by someone who can't write any better than this. She wonders if she is blushing. Why on earth did she make it so long? She could probably skip a few lines and nobody would notice. At last, the paper ends. The last line reads, "It isn't much of a car, but it's mine." Lois hates this line so much that she doesn't even read it.

The students stare at her in the silence. Wow, this feels awful. A few of them are smiling, but nobody says anything. Lois takes a deep breath. She looks right into the faces of two students seated across from her. They look relaxed; they're slouching. One is frowning. "Tell me about my paper," she begins. "Sum it up. What did you hear?"

The students look at one another nervously. Finally someone says, "It's a paper about making choices: how hard it is to get what you want when you don't have much money."

Someone else says, "I heard you saying that your car probably wouldn't look like much to anyone else, but to you it's still special."

Heads nod.

"OK," says Lois. She's moving too fast. She knows. She should let more of them respond before moving on, but she's still a little nervous. "Now, what struck you particularly? What stood out?"

Silence.

Lois wants to speak, to ask them, "Was it this part . . . or the part where . . .?" But she doesn't. She waits. Maybe they're a little nervous too.

Finally, one of them says, "I liked the part about how *you* chose the car; how you wouldn't let the salesman talk you into something you didn't like."

". . . the phrase 'ugly but functional.' "

More nods. Others comment. Lois is struck by how closely they have listened. One of them says, "I liked your comment . . . 'the security of driving my mess around with me. . . .' I couldn't imagine you driving in a messy car like that. That part was very funny."

"You didn't laugh, though," Lois remarks.

"I know—I didn't think we were supposed to laugh."

"OK, I think you're bringing up a good point here," Lois tells him. "We don't want to hurt anybody's feelings doing this, and we don't want to make anybody nervous or uncomfortable, but, on the other hand, I do need some sense of your reaction to what I'm reading. I feel nervous up here, too. Frankly, the silence was driving me crazy. I need to hear what you think and how you feel, OK?"

Lois reads through the paper again. She is more animated this time, her voice carries better, and she puts some feeling into it. Some parts are not quite so bad as she had thought the first time through. She even likes bits and pieces. Some of it is still pretty awful, but this doesn't seem so important all of a sudden. She reads the whole thing this time, last line and all.　■

Assessment Provides a Framework

Students who are experienced in assessing papers analytically never have to wonder what to say about a piece of writing. Phrases pop readily to mind. They learn to assess mentally as they hear a piece, and the responses they provide are explicit and useful. Furthermore, writers won't be wondering what is meant, because they'll have access to the same set of criteria. Lois and her students are getting there, but their communication is still a little awkward and disjointed. The awkwardness will diminish with time and practice.

In addition, given some experience with analytical assessment, Lois's students might say something like this: "The voice is strong, especially when you describe the car's interior. The imagery really works in that part. I'm a little confused about a central theme. I'm not sure I see what you're getting at. I wasn't convinced you really liked your car. The organization has some strengths; the introduction is especially good."

Will students really say this much? Will they really use this kind of language? Not at first, no, and not every time, but their combined comments will be impressive in their insight, thoroughness, and consistency.

How can assessment work in the most intimate student/teacher interaction—conferencing? Let's see.

INTERVENTION 3: CONFERENCING

Conferencing is a one-to-one discussion between student and teacher or between two students. Conferencing is an excellent teaching device, for a number of reasons. First, it tends to make student writers feel special. Everyone likes individual attention, a time when his or her piece of writing has center stage, even for a little while. Second, students who are reluctant to speak freely (or to speak at all) within a larger group will often open up in a conference. Finally, it gives you, the instructor, a chance to make specific comments relating to a given piece of writing, rather than trying to generalize to every student's needs. This is easier for you and usually more helpful to the student.

The purpose of conferencing is to give the student some very focused, personal feedback that will help him or her to assess a piece of writing and to see it from a different perspective. The student should come away from the conference with some idea about where the writing is going and what to do next.

Of course, there's one big problem with conferencing. It's time consuming. How on earth will you find the time to meet with so many students on a regular basis? Well, you won't if you make a big production of it. There are some shortcuts, though, that you can make without jeopardizing effectiveness.

First, keep in mind that a two-minute personal conference may be as valuable to a student as an entire hour spent in class, provided those two minutes offer some real direction for the writing. Plan to listen. A conference shouldn't be a minilecture. This is a waste of time for everyone. If you enter the conference with the idea that you'll hear some things you didn't expect to hear, both you and the student will enjoy yourselves, and even two minutes will be time well spent.

> If children don't speak about their writing, both teachers and children lose. Until the child speaks, nothing significant has happened in the writing conference (Graves, 1983, 97).

Some teachers find it helpful to read papers ahead of time and to make a few notes, but this isn't really necessary, especially if you remember that it's the student's needs and comments, not yours, that should drive the conference. Moreover, these are likely to take up time that you could better spend in other ways and to discourage you from doing conferences regularly. So, don't make notes, even if you feel nervous. Relax. Conferences get easier over time. Don't expect too much right away. The first time around, you're not likely to get a good response with a broad, general comment like "Tell me about your writing." That's when some specific questions like these can help:

If you were going to sum up your paper in a few words, what would you say?

What do you think you'll do next?

What is missing?

Is this the same paper you started to write? If not, tell me what happened.

How close is this piece to being finished? How do you know?

How would you like your reader to feel?

What could I tell you that would be most helpful right now?

Did you write this for yourself? If not, who are you writing for?

Tell me more about what happens between this paragraph (or section) and this one.

Tell me more about this character.

How do these two ideas fit together?

What have you learned while writing this? What new questions do you have?

Do you think the paper ends at the right spot? What happens right after it ends?

Does it begin at the right spot? What's happening just before this?

If you were writing this from the point of view of _____, how would it be different?

Where is the voice strongest? How do you know?

Pretend I wrote this. As a reader, what would you want to tell me?

Have you read it aloud? What parts do you like best?

Which parts were the hardest to write? Why do you think that is?

Tell me what you think the real strengths and weaknesses of this piece are.

You won't ask every question every time, naturally. The idea is to set your student thinking. You can do this by asking just one or two key questions each time, and then listening to what the writer has to say.

You can also ask students to assess papers analytically during a conference, with the understanding that such assessment is *not* conducted for the purpose of judging or grading but only to help the writer clarify how far the piece has come in the writing process and how far it still has to go. Classroom assessment's finest hour and highest purpose lie in its capacity to answer the question, "Where is this performance now in the process of 'becoming'?" Ideally, this is a question for teacher and student to answer together.

■ SCENARIO

Ed has been holding conferences with his students since the beginning of the school year. It's now January. He tries to conference with each student every two to three weeks, and, though it takes a fair amount of time, he feels the payoff is worth it.

The dynamics of the conferences are changing a bit. In the beginning, Ed had to ask lots of questions. Now, students usually come to a conference with things to say. Ed didn't intend for this to happen, particularly, and doesn't know what, if anything, he did to make it happen.

Jill has never been an exceptional writer. Until recently, she didn't like to write and wrote only when she was forced to. She didn't like talking about her writing, and her most frequent comment was, "I can't write."

At first, she didn't want to conference about her writing: "I have nothing to say about it. It's awful. I hate what I write."

The last two conferences, however, have been somewhat different. Jill is beginning to open up. She is writing more on her own. She keeps a journal. She is still, however, reluctant to voice opinions about her own writing; she looks to Ed for a lead. Today they're conferencing on a paper Jill wrote about her dog, Rafe. (See Figure 4.6.)

"What do you think of it? Pretty terrible, huh?" she asks him.

"What do *you* think of it?" he asks, tossing the question back to her. She doesn't answer right away, but Ed doesn't jump in to break the silence. The seconds tick by. Ed waits.

"I don't like the ending," Jill volunteers at last.

"Tell me about it."

"Well, it just stops. It doesn't tell how I really feel."

"How *do* you feel?"

She thinks for a minute. "Oh, it isn't like I miss him all the time. Some days I don't think about him at all. But then—well, it's like I'll see him at the door, or I'll see this shadow dashing around the side of the barn. Sometimes when we cook out, I think about him because he used

My Dog

Everyone has something important in their lives and the most important thing to me, up to now, has been my dog. His name was Rafe. My brother found him in an old barn where we were camping in a field near my grandpa's house. Somebody had left him there and he was very weak and close to being dead. But we nursed him back to health and my mom said we could keep him, at least for a while. That turned out to be for ten years.

Rafe was black and brown and had a long tail, floppy ears, and a short, fat face. He wasn't any special breed of dog. Most people probably wouldn't of thought he was that good looking but to us he was very special.

Rafe kept us amused alot with funny tricks. He would hide in the shadows and try to spook the chickens but they figured out he was just bluffing so he had to give up on that one.

When Rafe got hit by a truck I thought I would never stop crying. My brother misses him too, and my mom, but no one could miss him as much as I do.

FIGURE 4.6. Jill's Paper

to steal hot dogs off the grill, and one time my dad yelled at him when he did that and he slipped and burned one of his feet real bad."

"OK, these things you're telling me about Rafe—they're very real and personal—that's *voice*—and I can picture what you're saying, so that's *ideas,* too. You're giving the story some imagery and focus that I like very much. Do you think you might write about some of those things?"

"Do you think I should?"

"Well, when you were talking I had a much better sense of *you* in the story—of how much you missed your dog and how you thought about him."

"I think I could write about some of those things."

"How about if you give it a try, and we'll talk again in about a week?"

"How about the conventions and sentence structure? Were those OK?"

"Well, I'd like not to worry over that too much right now. Let's think about the ideas, the organization, the voice. You can always come back to the other. . . ."

"I don't want any mistakes, though."

"But is this the right time to worry about that?"

"I don't know; I just don't want to get a bad grade."

"OK," Ed nods. "Suppose we agree that for now, we'll *just* assess the three traits I mentioned: ideas, organization, and voice."

"That's all?"

Ed nods again. "And if you decide you want to publish this paper . . ."

"We can fix the other stuff, right?"

"*You* will have time to fix it, yes." ∎

INTERVENTION 4: REVISION

Tell any group of teachers in a workshop that revision is the key to good writing and you'll generally see hearty nods of agreement. The trouble is, so much energy has been spent on prewriting and drafting before we ever get there. Revision is like the last stop on a long, long vacation. Everybody is tired and really wants to get on home, even if it means missing a few things.

∎ SCENARIO

Cheryl and Francine are talking after class. They have a paper to revise for Monday. "How do you do it?" Francine asks.

"What?"

"Revise. How do you do it? What do you do?"

Cheryl shrugs. "I read it to my mother."

"And? What good does that do? What does she say?"

"Oh, she usually says something like, 'That's good, Sweetheart. Did you *really* write that?'"

"That's it? That's all that happens?"

"No, of course not. Then I ask her how to spell all the words I don't know. I ask her if I said anything that sounded really dumb, and she says no, not that she noticed, and then I go and recopy it." ■

Revision: What It Is

Recopying; fixing the errors: For many students, this is revision. If we want them to see it otherwise, we've got to show them what we mean by *seeing it again*. Show them the physical side of revision by sharing copies of revised texts; show them the mental revisioning by telling them stories about when, why, and how we have revised our own work.

There are no shortcuts. Learning to revise well takes years of practice and is never fully learned. If you haven't done a lot of it yourself, you're going to find it extraordinarily difficult to teach, so the first requirement in teaching students to revise is to write—often—and to revise what you write. There is no other way. If you do not, then you cannot talk with students about what real revising is like, and in all probability you and they will fall back upon the obvious: hunting down errors and rewriting the text to make it neat.

If you *do* write and revise, you will find the teaching of revision much easier because you will always have a story to tell and a revised text to share. Here are some other suggestions:

1. Get a hold of some revised work—your own or someone else's—and share the drafts at various stages with students. Let them comment on the differences they see. Figure 4.7 shows some revised text from an early version of the analytical scoring guide.

2. Make it clear with your examples that revising is something all writers do. It isn't only for incompetent writers who couldn't get it right the first time. It's for anyone who continues to think about and to process the text after the first draft has been done.

3. Help students understand revising in the sense of "revisioning" or seeing it again. Image building is a good exercise to illustrate this. Have students sketch or describe in writing one object or scene that they can picture clearly: a tree in the front yard; a potted plant; a chair. Ask them to close their eyes, return to the image, and see it again. What else is there? What did they miss the first time? Returning to the image helps them to see that revising means taking another look, which often, but not always, leads to changes, expansions, additions, or new directions. Younger students can do this exercise with pictures. In fact, working

The purpose of revision is not to correct but to discover (Calkins, 1986, 88).

5 paper (control)

~~Central idea and scope of paper are clear, whether stated or~~ *main idea or* ~~implied.~~ The writer organizes material to develop central idea. (The idea ~~is~~ *are* developed by examples, anecdotes, events that are clear and relevant.) The order may be conventional or not, but it is *move to ideas* discernible and moves the reader through the paper.

- Details are *ordered and* ~~effectively elaborated.~~ *relevant, working in a unified way.*

- Organization flows so smoothly that it is unnoticed.

- The reader can feel the beginning, middle and end as well as fullness of the writing.

- *Paper shows unity & cohesion.*

3 paper

The writer attempts to organ. material cohesively to dev. a centr. idea.

~~Central idea is reasonably clear~~ but scope and supporting material may not fully develop the idea. The writer may have missed opportunities for ~~elaboration.~~ ~~Ideas are organized but the pattern may seem forced or obvious.~~ *effective transitions.*

Ideas are org., but pattern may seem forced, obvious or incomplete

~~- The writer gets the job done but without energy or enthusiasm.~~

~~- There will be fewer details; they will tend to be general, predictable, or repetitive.~~

- The order may be ~~"forced or imposed"~~ —a conventional ~~format~~ *pattern,* ~~that's~~ perhaps (not) a graceful fit with the topic. *(e.g., forced)*

~~- The main ideas or events may not be supported as well as they should be.~~

1 paper

• Placement or relevance of some details may be questionable.

~~Central idea is~~ *disjointed* ~~vague,~~ poorly stated or ~~nonexistent.~~ Organization is haphazard or absent. Examples, details, events might not fit central idea.

~~- Examples, details, or events may not fit central idea.~~

~~- Development is scanty.~~

FIGURE 4.7. Sample Revision

with pictures is a good place for writers of all ages to start, because it helps them to see that revising and correcting are not the same thing.

4. Write and revise with your students, and let them see the results, even if you don't think they're good.

5. Separate a piece of writing (a student paper or some text you've taken from another source) into paragraphs, and ask students to piece it back together. Tell them to question every paragraph as they put it into a larger context: Does this paragraph belong here? Is it essential to the text at all? After a while, this questioning becomes automatic, and students can begin to pull paragraphs apart mentally, to experiment with new starting and ending points, and to see whether they can build connections where none existed before.

6. Ask students to talk in peer-support groups about their own experiences with revising, or ask them to write about *how* they revised and to share the written process in peer groups or with the whole class. The stories three students have told about their experience with revision follow.

CHLOE'S STORY (AGE 15)

I reread what I wrote and hated it. So I went out to play basketball with my brother and tried to forget about it. After dinner, I read it out loud. There were some parts that didn't sound like me, so I cut those out and redid the rest. I kept writing more than I needed and then chopping some off and what's left is my draft now.

BUD'S STORY (AGE 16)

I put off the revising part for as long as I could because I didn't really want to look at it again. Then when I reread it I was surprised it didn't sound as bad as I remembered. I started working backwards, with the end first, because that was the weakest part of the paper, so I wanted to put my energy into that. Then I cut it into pieces, with one paragraph or section in each piece, and laid them out on the dining room table and just played around with them for awhile, moving them different ways. And from this I figured out a new way to start my paper, but most of what I wrote the first time doesn't fit anymore.

DEIRDRE'S STORY (AGE 17)

After I read the paper to myself and thought about it quite a bit, I started talking out loud to myself about it. At first this felt funny, but then it started to be kind of fun. I would pretend someone was asking me questions about it, and I would answer them. (It's strange, but it was sort of like they were real people talking to me because I kept coming up with questions I didn't know I knew enough to ask. This is hard to describe!) It was easier talking than having to write everything down. As I was talking, I would think of new things to say though, so then I would have to hurry up and write those down so I wouldn't forget. Some of those notes didn't fit into my paper the way I wanted to rewrite it later, but a lot of them did and I used them when I revised my paper.

7. Let students revise a paper (individually or in pairs or groups) other then their own. Give *all* students the same paper, and then compare their revisions. Why did different writers go in different directions with their revisions? What features of the text or what connections and associations led them? Discuss these differences so that students know there is no one right way to revise and no single "right" answer. Help students respect the differences, for they are the beginnings of voice and the most valuable part of what each student writer has to share.

8. Make a bulletin board dedicated to revision as the heart of the writing process. Post some examples of revised texts by well-known authors. Post suggestions from students on techniques that work. Post samples of your own revised work or theirs.

9. Teach students to assess writing—their own and that of others—analytically. The ability to identify and to discuss strengths and weaknesses in writing provides the best foundation possible for building revision skills. What a writer can assess, he or she can begin to revise. The scores that a student might give to a text are not important. What matters is the student's sense of the relative strengths and weaknesses of the text as he or she talks about it: "Ideas are coming together but need more development." "This section is *irrelevant*; it sounds good, but it has to go." "Here the voice is strong. I like this." "The link between these ideas is weak; the conclusion goes off on a new topic and never ties things back in." "When I reread it, my mind wanders in this part. The voice must be weak here. . . ." However, don't encourage students to think that they are revising for a grade. This is a deadly trap. When students change their text to suit someone else, not themselves, they lose ownership of it, and the grade then loses its meaning in any case.

10. Start small. It's overwhelming for most students to imagine revising five-page themes. Work on revising one line or even *one word* within a line. Then, gradually, begin taking bigger bites.

11. Give students the freedom to start over or to just toss out what isn't working. Throwing away dead copy is among the most useful forms of revision.

12. Do revision and editing as a team. You can work on an overhead projector while students work on written copies of the same paper. Allow students to work individually at first. Then you edit on the

When we read, we introject the text into our inner life and at the same time project our inner life into the text. This is a heady interaction (Moffett, 1983, 59).

We learn to write primarily by building on our strengths, and it is important for the teacher to encourage the student to see what has potential, what has strength, what can be developed (Murray, 1985, 157).

The confidences to recognize what stands up well in a writing, what works, and what needs to be changed is not often a characteristic of student writers. They are used to dwelling on error and weakness (Mohr, 1984, 9).

overhead and respond to suggestions from the class. As you do so, students can compare their individual work with what the class as a whole has done.

A SHORT CHECKLIST

When assessment and writing processes exist in harmony, the student should feel confident responding to questions like these:

Which writing-process strategies will work best for me?

What do I need to do next?

What kind of feedback will help me most?

How would *I* assess what I have written?

THE MISSING STEP

The writing-process approach to teaching writing has great power, but often it leaves teachers with the vague feeling that something is missing. What's missing may be the sense of control that students gain from taking charge of their own work.

There are two ways to give students this sense of power. One is to ensure that the process itself is not too structured or too fraught with rules and times and attention to classroom management. Writers need freedom to start with drafting if they wish, to return to prewriting, to move ahead as they feel ready, and to use prewriting as a part of revision if this works, in short, to create their own personalized versions of the writing process, even if what they do looks chaotic to us. If it looks chaotic enough, it's probably working.

> Responses that encourage revision are those that offer support to the student writers as people, help them find their strengths as writers, set high standards for writing, and do all the preceding while encouraging them to become independent revisers (Mohr, 1984, 116).

The second way to empower students is to give them the means, the skills, and the opportunity to assess their own writing, not according to arbitrary rules but according to the value system and the criteria that the instructor and students generate together as an interpretive community. Students need to know what's working and why, as well as what isn't working and why. This doesn't mean that the criteria for evaluation must be fixed and permanent. They must grow and change with the vision of the writers who create them, but they must also, at any given time, be sufficiently clear that they can be expressed in writing, made public, and opened to discussion.

Peer review, conferencing, and other vehicles for providing feedback are all useful, provided that they do not foster too much dependence on outside validation. All writers need feedback from an audience and need to learn to use that feedback wisely. Yet, the most valuable thing any writer can have is a sense of him- or herself *as a writer.* This sense comes, ultimately, through revision—the ability to see and to believe in one's own truth. Skill in assessment gives the writer some measure of independence and enables him or her to say, "I will listen to you and weigh your opinion in balance with my own; but, ultimately, I will trust my own voice."

5

GRADING: WHAT
IT WILL AND
WILL NOT DO

- *We as human becomings are very cruel.*

- *There are a lot more reasons why I think hunger should not be a problem, but they just won't come out of my head onto the paper.*

- *For evil purposes, unfortold disruptances will occur.*

- *By the time one reaches his senior year of high school, he realizes that education is more important than it seemed to be in earlier years. Of course, by then, it is too late.*

- *It joyed my day.*

- *I know I went well off the subject, but I have good spelling.*

- *Think for one moment about just being dead. Plain dead. Doesn't start your heart beating with vigor, does it?*

- *He jumped into the solitude of his own room.*

- *Youth is one of the world's most precious resources. Though one of the few that once evaporated never condenses back again.*

- *Life is something anyone who reads this paper is experiencing.*

- **In my ebullience, the water now lapping against my calves did not consciously register danger.**
- **I slowed my pace to a sitting position.**
- **Our teacher that year was really strange, he would say that he could bring in dog's and cat's and they would do better than you.**
- **She called her something too terrible to put on this paper.**

■ SCENARIO

Gretchen is a freshman in Mr. Fields's English class. She has always received excellent grades in English and is known for her writing ability. She's just gotten back a research paper, the result of three weeks of work. It's a community-based research project on local health issues. In doing her research, Gretchen interviewed doctors, health administrators, nurses, patients, and other people in the community. She read books and toured several clinics. The research was, she felt, exceptionally thorough, and the paper was well written. Her grade: B+.

Today, she has come in for a conference with Mr. Fields about the paper. He listens carefully to what Gretchen has to say and agrees with her that her research methods were excellent. "I don't see what you're so upset about," he tells her. "In my class, a B+ is a very good grade—*very* good."

"Why isn't it an A?" she asks, trying not to sound too angry or hurt.

"An A paper is an exceptional piece of work."

"Why isn't this paper an A, though, or at least an A−?"

Mr. Fields sighs. He's trying to be patient, but she just isn't listening. "Gretchen, you did *very* good work, but, as I've said, for an A you have to do something, well, above and beyond."

"Like what?"

"Well, it isn't that easy to explain. Your paper, well, your paper was very close to an A, *very* close. It just needed that little something extra. You did a good job on the research and a good job of documenting that research. The paper was well written and flowed right along. It lacked a little zing or punch. Do you know what I'm saying?"

"But a B+ is so close to an A−!"

"Yes, it is."

"So, why couldn't this be an A− then? Why couldn't you change it to an A−?"

"Because it isn't an A−. It's a B+."   ■

What's missing in this teacher/student communication? Clearly, the teacher is unable to spell out for the student the meaning of a grade in terms of explicit performance criteria or to show her how he has applied criteria in making a judgment. He has, of course, used *some* criteria, but what are they? Is he considering Gretchen's past performance, past effort, or her attitude in class? Is he influenced by the topic? Is a B+ the top grade achievable in this class (the equivalent of an A in another class)? As long as questions like these remain unanswered, the teacher and student cannot communicate effectively.

WHAT ARE GRADES?

In Chapter 4 we talked about intervention that works—intervention being the teacher's way of jumping in at strategic moments to give students needed support or feedback. Donald Murray calls grades "the final intervention," meaning that once the grade is assigned, the paper's case is closed (Murray, 1985). Why? Well, a student who receives a good grade, or at least one that is acceptable, isn't likely to see the need to do anything further. On the other hand, a student who receives a C— isn't likely to think, "Boy, I'm going to turn this grade around, whatever it takes." Depending on how often this happens, the student is more likely to think, "What's the use? I can't write. No one ever likes what I write."

The moral of this story is: When you do assign a grade, you should be sure—and the student should be sure—that the piece of writing is finished, or, at least, as finished as the writer cares to make it for the time being.

Grades are meant to answer the question, "How effective is this piece?" To put this question another way, "Is this piece of writing establishing a connection between the writer and the reader?" The value of grades depends on the care with which they're assigned, the extent to which the giver and the receiver agree on the way grades are determined, and the mutual respect between the reader and the writer. It also depends a lot on *when* the grades are assigned. Feedback generally works best if the person who's receiving it has a chance to respond: to explain, to amplify, to defend, to clarify, or just to acknowledge how valuable the feedback was.

Grades rarely allow for this. They're usually final and permanent. Seldom, if ever, will a teacher seek a student's response to a grade; for example, "Did that B— seem appropriate to you?" This sounds too compromising to make some people comfortable. Yet, it's one of the best things a teacher can do, for it strips from a grade the cloak of authority to which it has no inherent right.

In the final analysis, grades are a form of personal response and cannot be more. If we're going to use them at all, we should be very honest with students about this. At the same time, it's also honest to acknowledge that in the real world, evaluations, even when they're

When I assign papers I should similarly start by advertising my gatekeeper role, by clearly communicating standards and criteria. That means not just talking theoretically about what I am looking for in an A paper and what drags a paper down to B or C or F, but rather passing out a couple of samples of each grade and talking concretely about what makes me give each one the grade I give it (Elbow, 1987, 154).

I can judge one of the main effects of personal grading by the attitudes of students who land in my remedial course in college. They hate and fear writing more than anything else they have had to do in school. . . . Apparently they have never written anything anyone thought was good. At least, no one ever *told* them that anything in their writing was good. All their teachers looked for were mistakes, and there are so many kinds of mistakes in writing that their students despair of ever learning to avoid them (Diederich, 1974, 21).

subjective, sometimes do count. Writers whose work no one wants to read generally don't get published—more than once anyhow.

This talk of subjectivity doesn't let us off the hook, though. Grades, like analytical scores, must be defensible, explainable, and based on known criteria that are themselves clear and important.

LET'S RECONSIDER GRADING

Surely no one would argue that grading systems are perfect. Anyone who's ever received grades or had to assign them knows the problems. Yet we live with them and tolerate them because we sometimes feel we have nothing better. We want a record of student performance, and we often believe, right or wrong, that students and their parents want such a record as well. Again, this may be a choice by default, the result of not knowing a better alternative. Also, we fear that if we didn't have grades the following might occur:

1. With the threat of low grades removed, students would not feel motivated to perform well.
2. Teachers would have no systematic means of keeping track of who is doing what and would have no ongoing record of which students perform best at various tasks.
3. Parents would look askance at a school system that didn't appear to track students' performance in any organized fashion.

If, for example, teachers see in their students competent, capable human beings, they seem to act in ways that naturally enable their students to explore, to grow, to stretch themselves beyond their own limitations. If they do not, if as a result of classroom problems or their own assumptions, students appear to them as incompetent or incapable, no technique or approach they use appears to be particularly effective. (Perl and Wilson, 1986, 258).

Would any of these things in fact occur if we didn't grade students? Only you can answer this question, but our view is that these fears are exaggerated. No doubt many students do write for the grade, which is a poor motivation at best. To suggest that they would not write if they didn't fear a poor grade is to say that there's no real pleasure in writing, that students will not write for the joy of it. This just isn't so. Given a workshop atmosphere in the classroom where writing is a way of life, given an instructor who likes writing and writes with the students, writing becomes not only pleasurable but irresistible. Students will not want to miss out. *Real* writer-reader interaction is exhilarating and soul-satisfying, for we all share a secret desire to let others in on what we think.

Would teachers lose track of students' performance? Not at all. In a writing workshop, assessment of student performance goes on all the time. Teachers and students read their papers, comment on them, and watch their evolution. Grades, which so often seem to be the apex of assessment, may be in fact only a poor substitute for *real* assessment or may bring the more valuable early assessment to a halt. When you grade a paper, you sign its death warrant, for the student will not review it again.

Will parents object? Not if they understand the reason for fewer grades. Some parents don't find grades valuable. The real clues to their children's performance, they contend, come when they hear them read stories that they've written and illustrated. In tales of outer-space picnics and snake hunts lie a hundred indicators about how young writers conceptualize, organize, and rethink ideas. No single grade can hope to communicate such richly varied information.

This chapter is not intended as a plea for abandoning grades altogether—necessarily. The reality is that teachers in most school systems are required to assign grades as part of an established record-keeping system, but grading should never be the sole focus or even the primary focus of a sound classroom-assessment system. Grades are one form of feedback but not the only (or even the most important) form. Having said this, let's acknowledge the fact that as a teacher of writing you probably *will* assign grades. So the real issue is not so much *whether* you grade as *how* you do it and what pains you take to ensure that grades are assigned and interpreted with care so that students understand what the grades mean and do not mean.

THE PURPOSE OF GRADES

Most educators would agree that we use grades to communicate. The teacher uses grades to send a message about student performance to students, parents, administrators, guidance counselors, and other teachers, as well as (sometimes) to employers, colleges, administrators, and others outside the school. It is extremely important that these messages be read accurately, that the symbols we use mean the same thing to the sender and the receiver. If we manage the feedback effectively, grades will serve their second important purpose: to encourage or to motivate students.

What does effective management of grading practices entail? First, grades must be linked to a public set of performance criteria, such as the analytical-scoring criteria we've been discussing. Second, specific procedures must be spelled out for translating performance ratings into grades. In short, students should have a clear idea of whether, how, and when each piece of writing will be graded and how grades (or other feedback) on individual samples of writing relate to an overall grade for the course as a whole.

POTENTIAL PROBLEMS WITH GRADES

Grading procedures lose effectiveness when they (1) begin to reflect student characteristics other than achievement, and (2) focus on achievement indicators that do not represent students' best performance. These problems can, however, be avoided if we're sufficiently careful in deciding whether, when, and how to assess.

What to Grade

Grades are subjective. This is no secret. But the point we've been making throughout this book is that subjective judgments can be made in a defensible and consistent manner. Here again, however, our goal should be to make them consistent and defensible by relating them to the highest quality objective measures of student performance available. If we base grades on the kind of writing assessment spelled out in Chapter 2, we can reach this goal. If we allow factors not directly related to writing performance to influence our judgment, however, we cloud the message that grades deliver.

Some teachers like to grade in part on the students' level of effort (e.g., rewarding the amount of writing done or the time spent rather than the quality of the writing). They believe this approach encourages hard work. We all value hard work, but if students receive the message via their grades that they don't have to perform as well as long as they *look like* they're trying hard, you can predict the result as well as we can. Besides, effort is a vague concept that can be difficult to measure objectively. If all teachers measure effort differently, we wind up making grades more subjective than ever.

What about basing grades on students' attitudes? Could we encourage better writing performance by rewarding a positive attitude toward writing? Probably we could to some extent, for some students, but again at a high cost. Attitude, like effort, is difficult to define and measure effectively. Is the student who fumes and frets and snaps pencils revealing a poor attitude about writing or only reflecting the reality of how frustrating writing can be sometimes? What does a positive attitude toward writing look like? How does it reveal itself, in and out of the classroom? Are we wise and vigilant enough to spot it when we see it? If not, then attitude assessments made by teachers in classrooms may reflect nothing but vague guesses.

Still other teachers like to take students' ability or aptitude into account. This means, in effect, rewarding overachievement and punishing underachievement. When aptitude is considered, the student of "low ability" might receive a higher grade on an equivalent piece of work than a student of "high ability," simply because the teacher holds different standards of performance for the two.

Now, on the surface, this approach appears to provide maximum motivation for both teacher and student, because it allows for realistic expectations, but here again, we must face up to the trade-offs. First of all, this concept of ability (or aptitude or intelligence) is a difficult concept to define and to measure effectively, even for educational psychologists who devote their careers to its study. How can we expect the classroom teacher to define and to assess ability objectively? The teacher may wind up relying either on the results of standardized performance tests (which, as we note in Chapter 1, tend to focus heavily on mechanics) or on past performance. What are the implications here?

Past grades, whether high or low, may unduly influence how an instructor "sees" current performance. It is human nature to question our own judgment when it deviates significantly from that of others. Traditionally "poor writers" (as defined by the grading system) may emerge at some point as shining stars. More often, however, grading patterns are self-perpetuating, because it's difficult to be objective about the performance of a student who "has always done well." (This is the very reason, by the way, that in large-scale writing assessments readers generally are not allowed to score papers written by students they know.)

We now have in hand a great deal of research on the effect of teacher expectations on student achievement. This research indicates that students will work up to the level that we expect them to achieve. Admittedly, we have to be careful not to set objectives beyond students' reach, but our expectations should rest on multiple indicators of students' potential capabilities (including our own judgment), as well as on an honest statement of what we truly value in writing performance.

There is only one acceptable basis for determining student grades in writing: careful, systematic analysis of students' actual achievement as measured against high-quality, agreed-upon criteria.

When to Grade

We feel that students should receive only periodic grades based on the teacher's evaluation of the highest-quality products that the student can produce. Students and teachers can work together in determining which papers will be graded, and, once the decision to grade a paper is made, the student may spend extra time editing and polishing it. Other pieces may be left incomplete, tossed away, or filed until the student feels motivated to revise them further. Such an approach not only increases the odds that grades will be based on students' best work but also parallels the way in which professional writers work. No writer finishes every piece. Some may be tucked away for years and then reworked. Some are thrown out. A few are taken all the way to publication, and these are the pieces that the writer spends time revising and editing.

This doesn't mean, however, that students should not receive feedback on other writing; they should. Such feedback can take the form of analytic scores and comments from fellow students and the teacher. It makes no sense, however, to grade work that is still in process. Drafting and revising should give beginning writers an opportunity to experiment, to take risks, and to try new things. During this time, it has to be OK to fail without sanctions. This means that there are no grades in the grade book. The best way in the world to keep students from growing as writers is to grade everything they do. When this happens, you can count on them to play it safe: Nothing ventured,

Students who worry about spelling too early tend to use familiar words and compose dull pieces of writing (Hansen, 1985, 185).

nothing gained. Good assessment doesn't hover. It steps in at the right moment, and then gets out of the way.

Now let's get specific. What role can and should holistic and analytical systems of writing assessment play in grading practices, and how should they be used?

ANOTHER GRADING OPTION: ANALYTICAL ASSESSMENT

We've already noted that grades do not mean the same thing to all students. They don't mean the same thing to all the teachers who assign them, either. Some teachers may view a B as an extremely strong grade, while others may see it as only moderately strong, far from impressive. Further, in responding to students' writing, any two teachers tend to focus on slightly different traits and mentally to weight them differently. One sees only the poor spelling, while another passes right over the mechanics, caught up in the ideas or voice. No wonder that teachers who grade a paper *without discussing* it rarely agree on what grade the piece should receive.

Remember the paper you graded in Chapter 4? Here it is again—a paper written by an eighth-grader about a friend who's important to him.

ERNIE, MY BEST FRIEND

Ernie is a fun person to be with, at least for me, and I cannot begin to recight all we did together. However I could give a few examples. For example, we used to swim in an old stone quarry over by his house. There was a tower in the pond that he used to haul himself up to the top of. Then I'd toss him a steel cable attached to a beam. He would then hurl himself into the deep green murk and disapear whith a splash. And what a splash! Once he swam the whole four hundred and twenty meters of the pond. He didn't even stop to pant.

We also went on skating parties together. He's the one who tried to teach me how to skate. I still don't know despite his efforts.

When we whern't swimming or skating we might have been playing Role Playing Games, our favorite pastime. It was not particularily mine though. He liked to play Gamma World, I liked Star Frontiers.

Ernie had a lot friends here despite his rather unsighly round stature. But when he moved to Ithaca he had trouble making friends. That was the biggest surprise of my life.

I suppose you need to know what Ernie looks like. Well his not the most beutifull frined in the world. he had a kind of amber colored eye. they were wide and kind eyes. Made you want to like him. he had a sort of blonde mix whith brown hair. That hair was always clean and striaght and stayed close to his head. he also a very tight color of skin that fit nicely around his bulbous bod. I suppose thats why he had trouble making friends down there because he was so large.

But he was my best friend, and always will be.

This paper has been presented to teachers in numerous workshops, and in most cases opinions are strongly divided. No one has ever given the paper a failing grade, but it has received everything from a D− through an A+. Occasionally, teachers split the grade and give one grade for mechanics and one for ideas or content. The ideas and content grade usually is always higher by one full grade and sometimes by two. Still, the diversity in responses suggests that for this writer at least, any grade received would be largely a matter of luck.

At the end of the workshop, once we've finished discussing all the reasons why the paper should receive this grade or that, someone will ask, "OK. What is it really?" (as if there *is a correct answer*). At that moment, it becomes strikingly clear how much power we assign to the grade giver. We must remember that a grade is just one person's truth. If we begin looking at it as *the* truth, we elevate it to a status that it doesn't deserve.

Do you recall what letter grade *you* gave this paper (in Chapter 4)? What grade would you give it now? As you make your decision, consider the message that a letter grade conveys to the writer: What does it tell (or neglect to tell) the writer? How could you enrich or strengthen the message?

For the sake of comparison, let's try scoring this paper according to the analytical scoring guide that we introduced in Chapter 2. Remember, it would receive one score on *each* of the six traits in that scoring guide: ideas and content, organization, voice, word choice, sentence structure, and conventions. Take a few moments to score the paper, and jot your scores down on a piece of scratch paper. Then turn the page and we'll share with you the scores that were provided by a group of trained raters and the rationales for those scores. As you review these scores (and reflect on your own), consider the nature of the message that analytical scoring provides.

Scoring the Paper

IDEAS AND CONTENT: 4

Most raters agree that the writer's purpose is clear and that the writer holds the reader's attention. The piece has focus. However, it lacks some sense of balance. Primary and secondary ideas vie for attention, and development isn't as strong as it might be. We'd like to know a little more about Ernie's personality: his sense of humor, perhaps, his devotion to the friend who's writing about him, the kindness that's hinted at but never brought to the fore. Still, we can picture him, we see him in action, and we have a strong, convincing sense of the writer's friendship.

ORGANIZATION: 3/4

Overall, strengths outweigh weaknesses, but, while the ideas and content score might be regarded as a 4+, the organization score is probably a 4− or a 3+. The introduction is not especially effective; it's just a warm-up for a writer who hasn't really started talking to us yet. The details, though often amusing, come at us a bit haphazardly; the order isn't as deliberate or as effective as it would be in a more carefully revised draft that might follow. It doesn't build purposefully to a revelation or a high point, and, as a result, the paper peaks too early with the splash into the quarry and takes too long winding down after that. The ending is traditional—not much of a surprise.

On the other hand, we don't get lost. The physical description of the friend is held off a bit until we know something about him and have begun to sketch him in our own heads; this is a nice touch. The pacing is good. The paper moves right along without dawdling. It stops very abruptly, but some readers consider this a plus.

VOICE: 4/5

Readers are generally divided here, but most agree that voice is the strength of the paper. This writer tells his story of friendship in his own way. The honesty of his feeling comes through; there's not a false note. Further, it's a likable paper. It is a paper that stands up to rereading because of its naturalness, its simplicity, and its warmth—a paper well suited to the friend it describes.

WORD CHOICE: 4

The language is individual, colorful, natural, and not overdone. Imagery is strong in most cases, though not consistently so. This writer doesn't rely on clichés. He's writing what he feels, and the words just come. Many readers have objected to the phrase "I cannot begin to recight [sic] all we did together." They think "recite" sounds stiff and forced. I don't agree; I think it works here.

SENTENCE FLUENCY: 4

You have to hear the sentences read aloud. You can't score the sentence flow and rhythm by looking at them unless you've got a very strong, clear reader's voice in your head. Read it aloud, or, better yet, have someone read it to you. You'll be struck, we think, with the variations in sentence structure and length. There are some awkward moments: "Ernie is a fun person to be with. . . ."; "I could give a few examples. For example, ..."; "he had a sort of blonde mix whith brown hair" (a good image but weakly constructed). However, this writer has some wonderful moments: "they were wide and kind eyes. Made you want to like him."

CONVENTIONS: 2/3

Conventions are the weakest trait of the paper. It suffers from faulty paragraphing, missing words, misspellings, improper capitalization, problem punctuation, and little things like uncrossed t's. The news isn't all bad. There are words spelled correctly: *attached, skating, despite, blonde, amber.* It's hard to know why a student who spells these words correctly has so much difficulty with *weren't:* "When we *whern't* swimming or skating. . . ." Spelling problems are often mysterious. Overall, weaknesses outweigh strengths somewhat, particularly if you think of how much editing would be needed to prepare this piece for publication.

What's the Message?

These analytical scores tell the writer that this is a developing paper with much promise, though it's far from being finished. The real strength of the piece is its voice, and this is as it should be early on. The word choice is also good: It's natural, and the imagery is strong. Ideas come through clearly, and the paper is interesting to read. The sentence structure has good rhythm, although some awkward moments break the stride. The organization needs some work. The introduction and conclusion aren't as effective as they might be, and, while the pacing is good overall, the climax of the piece comes too early, leaving things to wind down for over half the paper. (This is less noticeable than it might otherwise be, because this is a short piece.) Conventions are relatively weak, but the paper may not be ready for editing yet.

Where is this piece in terms of the writing process? It's well past the prewriting stage. Ideas are coming together and forming patterns. It's a draft (perhaps not the first) at some stage of revision. It's not a final draft, however. It isn't polished, and it isn't ready for publication. Moreover, this writer has more to tell—much more—if he chooses to do so. Therefore, grading the paper now doesn't make very much sense, but assessing it makes good sense. The assessment scores tell the student, relatively, where the strengths and the weaknesses lie and how far the paper has come along the continuum of development.

This assessment need not be done by the teacher. It might be done by the student writer. Furthermore, at this point in the writing process, because the draft is not final, conventions might not (probably should not) even be assessed.

Did your scores agree with those suggested? Remember that agreement is less important than your ability to defend your scores by using the criteria suggested in this scoring guide or your own criteria.

If you develop criteria of your own, they should be explicit. They should be written down so that everyone can see them, think about them, comment on them and make suggestions for improving or refining them. Notice that the purpose of *assessing* writing (as opposed to *grading* writing) is not to come up with *the* right answer or truth about a paper's value but rather

To explore how many "truths" come together to create a larger gestalt of meaning or reader response

To develop some consistency about the way in which we respond to writing

To set forth criteria that truly reflect what the teacher and the student writers value in writing

To provide a built-in framework for revising

To provide interim feedback *before* final grades are assigned, when there is still time and motivation to revise

To help show, through a comprehensive profile of strengths and weaknesses, where a piece is now in the writing process along a continuum from prewriting (in the sense of still playing with ideas) to the polished, finished stage (see the diagram below)

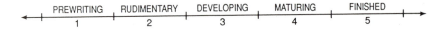

In classroom assessment, as in large-scale assessment, there's real value in having more than one person respond to a paper. When this happens, the resulting scores may be looked at as a range within which the "true" score probably lies. For example, if two teachers were to give Ernie a score of 4 and 5 on the trait of voice, we might reasonably conclude that the "true score" for voice lies somewhere between a 4 and a 5. This is another way of saying that the odds are, if 100 people responded to the paper about Ernie, most of them would rate the voice 4 or 5 and would be able to defend their ratings in a convincing manner by using the criteria in the scoring guide.

Our experience with large groups suggests that this kind of consistency is readily achievable. Where does this leave you? If grading is an accepted, established part of your district's record keeping, is there a way in which you can use analytical assessment and translate scores into grades? Yes, there is. Keep in mind that you won't be grading everything—perhaps only those pieces that have been taken all the way to publication. With this understanding, we will now discuss how you can translate analytical scores into grades *if* you wish to use them in that way.

TRANSLATING ANALYTICAL SCORES INTO GRADES

First, you need a specific set of "translation rules." You might develop these in collaboration with students. However, everyone must know in advance the level of achievement required to earn each grade.

Though it sounds strange perhaps to say so, it doesn't really matter what the specific rules are. It's easier to understand this once you recognize that any grading rules are by nature arbitrary, regardless of the subject matter. They can take many forms, but whatever form they take, they must answer one basic question: What performance is required for an A, B, and so forth on a particular piece of writing? Let's consider some alternatives for answering this question.

First, we'll consider grades on individual pieces of writing. Keep in mind that you do not have to assign a letter grade to *individual* papers in order to come up with a course grade. The alternative is to maintain ongoing records of actual performance ratings to be averaged and converted to a grade at report card time. Many writing teachers think it's better not to assign grades to each paper, because a single piece of writing gives such a limited picture of performance. If you do want or need to assign grades to individual papers, here are some options.

Regard the six 5-point analytical scales as contributors to a total assessment with a maximum score of 30 points. Cutoff scores for grades can then be fixed along this 30-point score scale; for example, if you attain 25 or more of the 30 points, you earn an A; if you attain 20 to 24 points, you earn a B, and so on. (Remember: These cutoffs are arbitrary. In your class a score of 22 might earn an A; in someone else's class, a score of 27 might be required to earn an A.)

Another option is to average ratings across the six scales and to fix the cutoff scores for grades in terms of this average: For example, if you attain an overall *average* rating of at least 4.0, you earn an A: if you attain an average rating of 3.0, you earn a B, and so on.

Note that a student who scores five 5s and one 1, for a total of 26, would have an *average* score across the six traits of 4.3 (26/6), which is strong indeed. Yet despite such a strong performance on most traits, some instructors might feel uncomfortable with the very weak performance on one trait. In this case, a slight variation on this option is to base the grade on an average but to allow no *single* score to fall below a minimum level, say, 2 or 3 or whatever the instructor (and, perhaps, student writers) feel is appropriate.

In evaluating writing, I know my grading system has to take into account all the abilities that come into play when a writer writes. Writing isn't one ability but a combination of many—experimenting, planning, choosing, questioning, anticipating, organizing, reading, listening, reviewing, editing, and on and on. (Atwell, 1987, 113-14).

A similar option is to look at the frequency with which students achieve certain ratings: For example, if five out of the six ratings are 4 or higher, the grade is an A; if three of six are 4 or higher, the grade is a B, and so on.

Note also that for any one of these alternatives or others you may be able to think of, you can vary the weight that you assign to any of the traits. For instance, if you've just completed an instructional unit on organization, you may wish to give this trait some extra weight in grading. On other occasions, you may wish to reduce the weight given to a particular trait or even to drop one or more traits altogether. It isn't necessary to score every trait every time. In fact, analytical scoring has the power to make grading very flexible. Remember, however, that if you vary the rules from time to time, you must be sure that students understand those variations thoroughly.

Again, it does not matter which way you choose to combine the various traits to define grading criteria, and it does not matter how or where you fix cutoff scores. These decisions are up to you. There are no rules of pedagogy or the psychology of human learning to guide you. Does this mean that you don't have to be concerned about fairness? On the contrary, it means just the opposite: You will need to be *very much* concerned with fairness. Since there are no rules to tell you whether the appropriate cutoff for an A is 22 points, 25 points, or 27 points, you will need to use your professional judgment in determining what expectations are fair and realistic—judgment that is based on review of numerous students' writing samples, on your own experience as a writer, on (we hope) regular and frequent discussions with colleagues, and on your own development and review of criteria for assessing writing.

If we give lip service to one set of criteria while applying another or if we keep our criteria secret so that students must guess how to succeed, we set them up for failure, and they have a right to feel resentful. The key is to hold up for students a stationary and highly visible target, one that will neither move nor disappear once they've taken aim and one that all agree is worth hitting in the first place.

USING ANALYTICAL ASSESSMENT AS A BASIS FOR GRADING

You may prefer to assess (but not to grade) individual pieces of writing and then use total scores to derive a grade at the end of the course or term. Here's one way in which it can be done. Keep a running tally of scores for all assignments that are rated (remembering that the student has some flexibility in determining which assignments will be rated). Your tally sheet might look something like the one shown in Figure 5.1. You can then total the scores at the end of the grading period and assign grades based on these totals. Again, as we noted earlier, you will need to determine cutoff scores for various grade levels. Notice that this approach allows you to rate each individual paper on one trait, two traits, or some other combination of traits that suits the current focus of your writing workshop. Holly's papers (Figure 5.1), for instance, are not all rated on all traits.

Tally sheets provide something concrete to show parents during conferences. Also, students can review the sheets and see where they've had their greatest successes and where they are consistently strong or weak. Such profiles are also useful to teachers, who may have an easier

Student's Name _Holly Day_

	Ideas and Content	Organization	Voice	Word Choice	Sentence Fluency	Conventions
Public Lab	1 2 3 4 5	1 2 3 4 5	1 2 3 4 5	1 2 3 4 5	1 2 3 ④ 5	1 2 3 4 5
Reports #5 & 6	1 2 3 4 5	1 2 3 4 5	1 2 3 4 5	1 2 3 4 5	1 2 3 4 5	1 2 3 4 ⑤
Writing assessment #1	1 2 3 ④ 5	1 2 ③ 4 5	1 2 3 ④ 5	1 2 3 ④ 5	1 2 ③ 4 5	1 2 ③ 4 5
Computers	1 2 3 4 5	1 2 3 4 5	1 2 3 4 5	1 2 3 4 5	1 2 3 4 ⑤	1 2 3 4 5
Amazing Ride *	1 2 3 4 ⑤	1 2 3 4 ⑤	1 2 3 4 ⑤	1 2 3 4 ⑤	1 2 3 ④ 5	1 2 ③ 4 5
Baseball	1 2 3 4 5	1 2 3 4 5	1 2 3 4 5	1 2 3 4 5	1 2 3 ④ 5	1 2 3 4 5
Autobiography	1 2 3 4 5	1 2 3 4 5	1 2 3 4 ⑤	1 2 3 4 5	1 2 3 ④ 5	1 2 3 4 5
Poster	1 2 3 4 5	1 2 3 4 5	1 2 3 4 5	1 2 3 4 5	1 2 3 4 5	1 2 3 4 ⑤
"Cinquain"	1 2 3 4 5	1 2 3 4 5	1 2 3 4 5	1 2 3 4 ⑤	1 2 3 4 5	1 2 3 4 ⑤
Poetry	1 2 3 4 5	1 2 3 4 5	1 2 3 4 5	1 2 3 4 5	1 2 3 4 5	1 2 3 4 5
Pet Essays	1 2 3 4 5	1 2 3 4 5	1 2 3 4 5	1 2 3 4 5	1 2 3 4 5	1 2 3 4 5
Social Studies Research	1 2 3 ④ 5	1 2 ③ 4 5	1 2 ③ 4 5	1 2 ③ 4 5	1 2 ③ 4 5	1 2 3 4 ⑤
Science Research	1 2 3 ④ 5	1 2 3 ④ 5	1 2 3 ④ 5	1 2 3 ④ 5	1 2 3 ④ 5	1 2 3 ④ 5
Term 2 assessment	1 2 3 4 5	1 2 3 4 5	1 2 3 4 5	1 2 3 4 5	1 2 3 4 5	1 2 3 4 5
TV Review	1 2 3 4 5	1 2 3 4 5	1 2 3 4 ⑤	1 2 3 4 5	1 2 3 4 5	1 2 3 4 5
Space Report	1 2 3 ④ 5	1 2 3 ④ 5	1 2 3 ④ 5	1 2 3 ④ 5	1 2 3 ④ 5	1 2 3 ④ 5
	1 2 3 4 5	1 2 3 4 5	1 2 3 4 5	1 2 3 4 5	1 2 3 4 5	1 2 3 4 5
	1 2 3 4 5	1 2 3 4 5	1 2 3 4 5	1 2 3 4 5	1 2 3 4 5	1 2 3 4 5
	1 2 3 4 5	1 2 3 4 5	1 2 3 4 5	1 2 3 4 5	1 2 3 4 5	1 2 3 4 5
	1 2 3 4 5	1 2 3 4 5	1 2 3 4 5	1 2 3 4 5	1 2 3 4 5	1 2 3 4 5

* Amazing Ride : Witch paragraphs

FIGURE 5.1. Tally Sheet for Analytical Assessment

(Source: Reprinted with permission of Ronda Woodruff, Beaverton (OR) School District.)

time planning instruction if they know, for instance, that students are writing with strong voice but are struggling with organization and syntax.

You may be wondering whether holistic assessment would work as well—with less time invested. The answer is no, not really. Holistic assessment is really very similar to grading. This is one reason that teachers, who often work as holistic raters, learn it very quickly and feel at home with it almost at once: They're using numbers instead of letters, but the process as a whole is very familiar.

In the general-impression version of holistic assessment, as we've mentioned earlier, papers are grouped from strongest (overall) to weakest performance; then the scores are assigned accordingly. Theoretically (though this rarely happens), the "best" paper in a group of papers might not be a particularly successful paper in its own right; yet in a holistic system, it could receive the highest score just because it is the best of the bunch, whether it is effective or not. Similarly, the "poorest" paper might actually be a fairly strong piece yet receive a relatively low score simply because other papers were judged to be even *more* successful. Few teachers feel comfortable assigning grades on this basis, even though, in reality, the best performance out of a large group is usually quite good, and the poorest usually has some significant problems.

If using general-impression scoring as a basis for grading makes us a little uncomfortable, what about focused holistic scoring, in which the criteria for scoring are well defined? Well, at first glance it looks better, admittedly, but again, think of the message to students. What does a holistic score *mean* to the writer who receives it? It is hard to say whether a score of 3, for instance, signifies strong ideas but weak conventions or impeccably edited prose that is also dry and dull.

Further, because it is extraordinarily difficult to attend to many traits at once, there is no way to feel confident that a holistic score reflects a balanced response to all traits. We all have biases. If we care more about voice than any other trait, what's to keep us from giving a holistic score of 5 to a paper that has a powerful voice but little else of merit? In analytical scoring, we can respond *just* to voice (with a score of 5) and then, having gotten this out of our system, move on to consider other traits.

When analytical scores are translated into a grade, these scores do not need to go away; they become part of a record somewhere—a record to which students, parents, and educators can turn to see what the grade means in fine print, broken down into components. Holistic scoring does not enrich the message of the grade; it merely provides a parallel message in numbers instead of letters. Converting holistic scores to grades is like going from Celsius to Fahrenheit: It's the same information, just stated a little differently.

WHAT TO TELL PARENTS

Parents are used to letter grades. Now, suddenly, here you are with numerical scores, scoring guides, strengths and weaknesses, continuums, and the rest. How do you explain it all?

Perhaps the best way, if you have the luxury of time in which to do it, is to have parents write a short piece during back-to-school night, grade it themselves, then score it, and consider the contrasting kinds of information that these two assessment procedures can provide.

Expect parents to be horrified, at first, at the thought of having to write. You can assure them that they will not have to read their writing aloud or to show it to anyone else unless they want to. It's important, however, that they work with their own writing. Because they have a personal investment in it, they will care about how it's going to be assessed. Parents have feelings, too.

As writers (if only for a night), they will quickly identify with the students' need for sensitive, good assessment, and they will quickly perceive the value of getting feedback during revision while there is still an opportunity to make use of it. They will also appreciate the value of narrative feedback—something that goes beyond just a number or a letter grade.

> Imagine the sorry results of an infant trying to learn to speak by a process equivalent to our freshmen English or writing courses (Elbow, 1987, 73).

When you are introducing parents to the six traits (or however many you might use within your own class), start with a simplified version of the scoring guide, if possible. It probably won't be as complete or as impressive as the other version, but it can be skimmed quickly, and you can always hand out the other as a backup if you like. Figure 5.2 is a simplified version of a scoring guide, redone in the form of a series of questions. It's intended for use by students as they review and revise their work, but its simple, clean format makes it a good model for introducing analytical assessment to parents.

The purpose of this introduction isn't to train parents as raters or to make them sophisticated evaluators of writing. The purpose is simply to acquaint them with analytical assessment, to introduce them to the traits you'll be teaching and using with your student writers, and to help them understand what the numerical scores mean.

You can also explain that student writers will be learning to score their own writing and that of other students and that sometimes they will score outside writing and your writing. Add that not every trait will be scored every time and that some papers will be coming home marked *Draft*; these will not be scored or graded on conventions because they're not yet finished.

Also explain that your students, like professional writers, will have publication as their goal, so they may be posting their writing on a bulletin board, sharing it orally, or making books. If you have sample books, this is a good time to show them. Add that selected pieces,

PLEASE KEEP TAPED ON YOUR DESK

*Questions for *Revising and Editing*

*Ideas/Content

1. Do my ideas work together to make my message clear?

2. Do I have enough information?

*Organization

1. Does my paper have an effective introduction and conclusion?

2. Do my words, phrases, and sentences tie my ideas together logically? (Transitions)

3. Are my ideas written in order of importance?

*Voice/Tone/Flavor

1. Is there evidence that I am sincere and concerned about my audience?

2. Is my paper an example of my best effort?

*Word Choice

1. Are my words accurate, concise, and well chosen?

2. Do I feel the need to experiment with any new words?

3. Is my paper enjoyable to read?

*Syntax/Sentences

1. Are my sentences varied?

2. Does my writing flow naturally?

*Writing Conventions

1. Is my paragraphing sound?

2. Does my punctuation enhance the meaning?

3. Have I checked my spelling?

4. Are my capitals where they belong?

5. Do I have subject/verb agreement?

FIGURE 5.2. Simplified Scoring Guide

(SOURCE:. Reprinted with permission from Ronda Woodruff, Beaverton (OR) School District.)

chosen by you and the students together, will be graded according to preset rules, based on assessment scores in various combinations. In other words, some papers may be scored (and graded) on two or three traits, some on four, and some on five or all six.

Don't forget to point out that your students, not you, will take responsibility for their own writing. You and your students will score and discuss conventions in class. You will give students numerous opportunities to practice their editing skills on their own writing and pieces of outside writing, but you will not be editing for the students. This will be *their* job.

Remember, it's invaluable to share samples of your students' writing if you have them. You might even try having parents score papers (informally) so that they can compare their responses with yours and your students'.

Nothing takes the place of a personal introduction, but it's also very useful to have a good letter to send home that explains to parents something about your philosophy of and approach toward writing instruction. Here's an example:

SAMPLE LETTER TO PARENTS

September 10, 1985

Dear Parent(s):

I believe that writing is an important basic tool for learning, self-discovery, and communication. Writing helps students learn to think more clearly and to order their thoughts. Through writing, individuals can express personal ideas, attitudes, and feelings that then can be examined by the writer and others.

Writing is a process and must be taught that way. Instruction this next year will focus not only on what students produce but also on how they compose. The writing stages include: prewriting (experiencing, observing, generating ideas, researching, and planning), drafting (expanding, organizing ideas), revising (assessing and reshaping content), editing (proofreading), publishing or sharing, and audience response, as well as evaluation methods consistent with writing as a process. Instruction in grammar, usage, and mechanics will be emphasized at the editing stage.

Students will have the opportunity to write frequently in a variety of forms for different purposes and audiences. Writing is a skill that students will use in all curriculum areas, not just language arts. Students will not only learn to write but also write to learn.

Good writing occurs in a climate of trust and acceptance where both personal expression and development of ideas are valued. Students will have ample opportunity to read their writing aloud, to assess and discuss their writing, and to work with their peers in composing and editing.

Please come to visit and feel free at any time to call me if you have questions concerning our writing program or your child's individual progress.

Sincerely,
(Signature)

(SOURCE: Adapted from a longer original and reprinted with permission from Ronda Woodruff, Beaverton (OR) School District.)

PRIORITY 1: FEEDBACK THAT MAKES SENSE

Analytical assessment, if it is based on sound, well-defined, valued criteria, is less arbitrary than most forms of grading, and it suggests to students some of the things that are important in good writing. To write well, you must read well. Assessment teaches a student to read with a critic's eye—and something of a critic's heart as well—separating the writing from the writer and learning to view it objectively.

If, suddenly, the admissions process were to become noncompetitive, the need for grading would vanish. But the need for evaluation would remain (Bleich, 1975, 105).

If they're going to get better at their craft, student writers need answers to two questions: Are you understanding this? Are you liking it? Grades provide minimal feedback, but often it comes too late and tells too little. A C— says that something went wrong; often it's up to the student writer to figure out what. Comments help, but few teachers have time to write more than a line or two. An analytical scoring guide, if it's well done, is a compilation of comments that, although they will not fit each piece of writing perfectly, offer a very good indication of the probable strengths and weaknesses. The teacher can then focus on the positive, offering one specific comment that relates to the story or the argument at hand.

The scoring guide presented in Chapter 2 is intended as a model. We believe it's a good one, and the thousands of teachers who have used it (or a version of it) have found that it works well also. Nevertheless, as a teacher with your own values, your own students, and your own teaching philosophy, you need the freedom to develop a scoring guide that works for you. This guide might offer a place to start. Yet there could be parts that you'd like to change. You might wish to add new criteria or to start your own list from scratch. We encourage you to do that, and Chapter 7 shows you how to go about it.

6

THE TEACHER AS WRITER

- Kate is like a stuffed animal that you get attached to you.
- We would sit together crying till our eyes were blue.
- We care about our appearance and take showers daily and comb our hair quite often.
- We were too young to have problems, so we talked about when we grow older.
- With her I can secede in my life.
- A special person inside and out he was.
- About five weeks ago we lost Jenny. She didn't die, but it is the next worst thing. She moved.
- He does not offend other people for what they are.
- When we got in trouble, our mom would become a taxi and take us to the golf course.
- She is just like me in a different way.
- He is not only a friend but a graven image.
- Amsterdam was more cultural than Hawaii, but it was still a lot of fun.
- There is always chaos in what we are doing.
- Her eyes are two different colors, brown and green, so you can always tell if it's her or not.
- Why does time take so long to happen?

When you first thought about being a writing teacher, did you picture yourself writing? I didn't. I envisioned myself handing out assignments, being the one with the power for a change, making the important decisions: how many words would be required, what the topic would be, when it would be due, whether rough drafts would have to be turned in with the final copy, whether spelling would count, and so forth. Basking in the glow of this newfound power, I certainly handed out my share of inane assignments with meaningless parameters. Did any of the requirements make sense? I certainly didn't know. I didn't have to be very concerned about it, either, since I wasn't responsible for the writing; I was responsible (at last!) only for making the rules and judging the results.

Then one day, a student asked where I had gotten my ideas for writing, how I knew how long the papers should be, and how many drafts I usually wrote. How many drafts? Why, none.

I wasn't writing drafts; I was *assigning* drafts. So how did I know it would take 500 words to "describe an important friend in your life"? I was a teacher. I *had* to know. Writing teachers are born with an instinct about these things. My writing teachers always knew. They had modeled precisely what I was doing—the handing out of assignments. And I had learned that script very well. It was amazing, in fact, how rapidly I began to sound as if I'd been handing out assignments all my life. . . . "For Monday, we'll do two pages on a favorite place. . . . For next Friday, 500 words on an experience you'll never forget. . . ."

But was I really teaching writing? I certainly thought so then. I no longer think so.

As a giver of assignments, I was neglecting to do the single most important thing a writing teacher can do: write. Oh, yes, I wrote letters to friends, of course, and articles for a local newsletter, which were enough to reassure myself that I could still string sentences together, but I wasn't really writing—not in the way I was asking my students to write. Why? Because this wasn't the way I'd been taught. Not one of my writing teachers had ever modeled writing. Did they write? I don't know. Did they know how to write? I couldn't say, to this day. They reviewed my writing and evaluated it, and I believed what they said, although I never saw one of them write anything other than cryptic marginal comments like "awk, "frag," and "dic."Children are trusting.

Later, I started feeling uneasy. Why was it that all those teachers who had said writing was so important didn't write? Maybe I wasn't being as tough on myself as I ought to be. Would I be asking my students about *Hamlet* if I hadn't read the play? That would be ridiculous and presumptuous, and everyone would see it as ridiculous and presumptuous. You couldn't teach literature if you weren't a reader.

No one, however, was calling me ridiculous or presumptuous for teaching writing without being a writer. I decided that before someone did, I would be ready to say, "Yes, you bet, I write all the time." Would it make me a better teacher? I wasn't sure.

I started to write with my students on practically every assignment. When I wanted to give them some extra work on revision, I wrote a paper and we revised it together. They liked it. So did I. Gradually, the whole feel, the whole texture of the course changed. My students began to notice the writing when we talked about literature. They didn't just talk about themes and plots and characters. They talked about the way sentences were structured and whether introductions were effective or the imagery worked, whether the organization made sense or the text stopped short and left them dangling. They talked about whether the writing was believable. They became opinionated.

Then they started asking questions about their own writing: What's a good way to start a paper? How much can you tell the reader before it's too much? What's the difference between a colon and a semicolon? What's wrong with having a one-sentence paragraph? If topic sentences are so great, why don't other writers use them? What's wrong with fragments? (Other writers are using them.) Why do we define sentences as "complete thoughts"? Some fragments seem like complete thoughts.

They asked me some questions I couldn't answer (What's wrong with "the reason is because"?). Maybe I should have been embarrassed by this, but I wasn't. It seemed like a real plus having students who would make me stretch, too. I figured that if I couldn't answer every question in that class, at least this would give the students a reason to come back next time (after I'd had a chance to bone up).

Some questions were the kind that you just have to think about. Some questions had answers we could look up. We started to bring handbooks and dictionaries to class so that we could learn together. We kept on writing. We kept on revising. We worked in small groups and turned ourselves into critics and reviewers. The students became far more skillful at this than I would have thought possible. I had underestimated their skill.

They showed good judgment in identifying writing that worked, and they began to be more articulate, listening to one another and defending their points of view. (At this point, it didn't occur to me to formalize their comments in the form of a scoring guide; this bit of wisdom would come much later.) Some of them wrote better than I did, and they knew it. They felt good about it, and so did I. Something else happened. We began to develop a sense of ourselves as a community of writers. The gap between us narrowed. Also, I discovered, to my surprise, that not only is power not essential to good teaching, it's a detriment.

WRITING WITH STUDENTS: RESEARCH SUPPORTS IT

Growing numbers of teachers are discovering the joys (and agonies) of writing with their students. And research is showing that teachers of writing, if they wish to be effective, must themselves write (Graves,

[Successful] Teachers write and share their writing, processes and products, with their students. They personally experience what they ask of student writers, from finding a topic through going public. Teachers do not require student writers to do anything they don't do themselves as writers (Atwell, 1987, 283).

1983; Murray, 1985; Calkins, 1986; and Atwell, 1987). Why is this true? What difference does it make?

Let's start with logic. Who among us would dream of having our children take piano lessons from someone who couldn't read music or swimming lessons from someone who couldn't float? Of course, we take a lot for granted. It saves time. Some people might look good parading back and forth at poolside, their whistles swinging from their necks, but what will happen when Johnny gets in over his head and goes under? We had better hope that the teacher can do more than blow a whistle.

■ SCENARIO

Alice has been teaching writing for about thirty years. She suspects that the big problem with today's students is that they're pampered too much, and some of this she blames on the "writing-process approach that eases kids into writing, although what they really need to do is to plunge right in and do it, the way we had to."

Alice believes in having students do lots of writing: "Practice is the key." She gives at least one assignment a week, usually on a Friday, so that students have plenty of time to work over the weekend and no excuses for coming in Monday with nothing done. Sometimes they disappoint her by doing just this, but at least she is giving them every chance.

Increasingly, she's been dismayed at how little students seem to retain despite lengthy explanations and extensive drills. It's maddening, really. "What's most disheartening," she tells a colleague, "is that they just don't seem to get the *point* of the assignment. I ask for one thing, and I end up getting something totally different. Not what I expected at all. They don't listen, and sometimes—I hate to say this, and ten years ago I wouldn't have—but they just don't try. It drives me crazy. When I was learning to write, we had to get it right. I mean we *had* to. We cared about our grades, and we tried hard to write what the teacher wanted. We couldn't get out of school without learning to write."

Alice has never written with her students and has no intention of starting now. "What's the point?" she says. "I *know* how to write. I'm not the one who is learning how to write; *they* are. I learned to write thirty-five years ago, and I was very good at it, by the way. That's why I'm here." Alice has hard evidence to back up her claims. She has saved quite a few of her old term papers and other assignments. She received A's on almost all of them and now and then a B+ but nothing lower, ever, so, of course, she wouldn't find much challenge in responding to her own assignments, would she? ■

REASONS FOR NOT WRITING WITH YOUR STUDENTS

We'll discuss why it's good to write with your students in just a minute, but, for now, let's consider a few reasons for *not* writing with students. You can probably think up a number of your own, or you could use one of these.

Reason 1: I know how to write

Sometimes people have the notion that learning to write is like learning to ride a bike: Once you know it, you never forget it. Some of these people, like Alice in the previous scenario, never do much writing after they get out of college. Why bother, they say to themselves; I've mastered it, haven't I? My grades and the approval from many writing instructors prove it.

It's just this sort of logic that makes thinking people question the value of assessment. The inference is that a grade (which is a kind of assessment) reflects overall writing ability, although, in fact, the most a grade or any assessment can do is to evaluate a particular performance. That evaluation might look very different on another day, or given another assignment, another evaluator, or another set of criteria. Furthermore, writing isn't something you learn once and for all. The struggle is forever, even for the Alices among us.

Of course, it is possible to reach a certain minimum competency level (a level at which it's simple to dash off a note about canceling a lunch date or to write a letter requesting a mail-order catalog, or to fill out an application for a job). But let's get serious here. Is this what we mean by writing? Filling out an application for a job looks a lot like writing maybe, but it isn't writing. It's form filling. If we want students who are competent in form filling or note writing, let's teach classes in that. If we want students who can write, let's offer classes in real writing, taught by people who can tell students what to do when they get stuck because they've been there. Recently.

Reason 2: I'll have to be wonderful

Let's make a distinction here. It's important for teachers to write with their students; it isn't imperative for teachers to be Anne Tyler or Maya Angelou or Tom Wolfe. There's a lot to be learned and shared this side of genius. Maybe there's Pulitzer Prize material in you and maybe not. If there is not, you can console yourself with the fact that the most gifted writers are not necessarily the best teachers. Teaching is an art in itself. However, the best teachers of writing are themselves writers at some level, in some way. They aren't always successful at it. They aren't always thrilled with what they write, but they *do* it.

I can't overemphasize how important it is for teachers of writing to write themselves. Albert Einstein once said regarding science that "the years of anxious searching in the dark, with their intense longing, their alterations of confidence and exhaustion and the final emergence into the light—only those who have experienced it can understand it" (Ziegler, 1981, 5).

Doing it and continuing to do it—this is the key. It's easy to forget how tough it is. It's easy to think that if you did it well once you can do it well anytime. Don't kid yourself. Doing it well once demonstrates potential. It doesn't stamp you as permanently publishable. It does, however, offer you some clues about how to get there again—clues you can share with your students.

Always there's the haunting fear: Suppose I do it and not only is it not wonderful but it's a downright disaster—unfit to read. Don't despair. Muster a little courage: you can give your students invaluable insight by sharing what you've learned from your own failures. Think how human you'll seem and how relieved they'll be to discover that published writers really are made, not born.

You can also take some comfort in knowing that you don't have to be consistently brilliant. Failure, like success, comes and goes. Poor writing isn't a hanging offense. Anyway, who would you want for your teacher—someone who outshines you at every turn; someone whose relentless genius leaves you perpetually thunderstruck; or someone who will show you, honestly, what success and failure both look like, how to tell the two apart, and how to get from one to the other?

Reason 3: I don't have time

The notion of the writer who takes long walks on sandy beaches and sits atop a cliff waiting for sea spray and inspiration to strike is a myth. Professional writers snatch bits of time here and there and make do. They get up early, go to bed late, give up weekends and evenings, write while others are showering, phoning, or watching television. They manufacture privacy on their decks, in their bathrooms, in their laundry rooms, and in the back seats of their cars. There is never enough time.

Most of us probably wouldn't find time to eat either, if we didn't enjoy it. If you want to be a writing teacher, you must love it enough to make time for it. It isn't easy, so you will need to improvise. Give up something else: vocabulary drills; spelling; worksheet time; announcements (post them).

Interweave your writing with other content instruction. Write about mathematics, geography, psychology, social studies, or chemistry. Write while students are writing. In a writing workshop, you're going to allow some time for drafting. You can take five or ten minutes of this time (or a bit more) for your own writing, during which you can ask students not to interrupt you. What they lose by having you inaccessible to them during this short period of time they will gain by seeing a real-life writer at work, one who takes the work seriously. If it isn't important enough to do, why is it important enough to assign? Next time you hear yourself saying, "I'd write with my students, but I just don't have time," ask yourself how you would respond to a student who said that to you.

REASONS TO WRITE WITH YOUR STUDENTS

Good things will happen to you and to your students if you write with them. Here are a few of the advantages in writing noted by teachers who write with their students.

1. *You'll teach by example, by providing a model of a writer at work.* "Show me; don't tell me," we say to students. We need to do this too. Students need to see us wrestling with ideas, making connections, starting off one way and then taking a new turn, mercilessly hacking off chunks that don't work, clarifying, using resources (dictionaries, textbooks, handbooks, writing of theorists and critics), sharing, rejecting, finding the right word, learning as we go, succeeding, failing, and overcoming the failure. The more we share, the more they will learn.

2. *You'll learn that some assignments aren't worth doing.* When students do not perform well or do not do what you have expected, sometimes it's the fault of the assignment: it wasn't clear; it was too broad, too narrow, or too irrelevant; or it was a dumb idea. Good assignments are hard to create. Students generally write better if they're allowed to select their own topics or, at least, their own way of pursuing a particular topic. This increases the chances that they'll care about what they write, and caring makes for better writing.

Some students feel lost without an assigned topic. We have taught them, sadly, that coming up with a topic is not part of the student writer's responsibility. For these students, should you make assignments? If you do, you perpetuate their dependency. They will pressure you to hand them a topic. Resist. The texts you are working with in literature and other content areas should suggest to you and to your students many potential topics. Give students an opportunity to explore several of these topics in various ways—through reading, writing, and talking with others. Encourage them to write down the questions that arise through this exploration. Posing and answering their own questions provides a good basis for involved writing. We care most about our own questions, not those someone else has posed to us.

Children who are fed topics, story starters, lead sentences, even opening paragraphs as a steady diet for three or four years, rightfully panic when topics have to come from them. The anxiety is not unlike that of the child whose mother has just turned off the television set. "Now what do I do?" bellows the child (Graves, 1983, 21).

Remember, too, that finding your own way into and out of a topic is part of what it means to write well. When we box students in with overstructured assignments, we cheat them of the opportunity to develop this important skill. We must decide, though, what it is we want: a voiceless litany, responding to a single question (ours) or thirty different sets of questions, each with its own answer.

3. *You'll learn why some writing turns out very differently from what you expect.* How many times have you gone to the grocery store intending to buy just one thing and wound up with a whole carload of things that you didn't even know you needed? Good writing is equally unpredictable. Professional writers know this because they see it happening before their eyes. Student writers see it happening too, only they often think that they're doing something wrong—getting off the topic, we call it.

Often this tendency to wander is the result of thinking at work; it's the writer making connections that may lead into some interesting territory far more worthy of exploration than the path already started.

Unfortunately, people who create writing assignments, unless they're writers themselves, don't recognize the value of exploration. When they create an assignment, the expected result is generally well mapped out in their heads. If the student's response doesn't match their expectations, they may not be pleased. If they're not pleased, they won't encourage future exploration.

We do not teach writing effectively if we try to make all students and all writing the same. We must seek, nurture, develop, and reward difference (Murray, 1985, 5).

As you write you'll find that making connections as you go is half the fun, once you're convinced that your own idea can teach you something. You'll take a more intrepid view of charting new territory and will grow increasingly disenchanted with predicting results for yourself or for your students. Of course, you'll have to give up the security that comes with getting thirty papers that sound like clones of one another.

4. *You'll get in touch with the process of revision.* Lots of teachers go as far as doing prewriting with their students. Prewriting is fun; it's easy; and it's fast. However, while it's often a valuable step for the writer who needs to get going, in some ways it's still on the fringes of real writing. Student writers need us to share more than the latest brainstorming technique. They need to see how it looks and feels for writers to make connections through the creation of a whole text.

Prewriting gives us associations and clues about where to go. In creating and sharing text, we learn how ideas are shaped and reshaped in our minds. We see where we're going and where we've been. In hearing what others have written, we make new connections that allow us to "re-vision" ideas so that our revisions reflect our thinking. As a writer, you can share the story of how your ideas have evolved and what they're teaching you. If you do not write, you'll have no story to tell.

5. *You'll find yourself becoming more sensitive to evaluation and assessment, because you'll be going through it too.* As the old saying goes, everything is easy to those who don't have to do it themselves. Writing makes for a dangerous spectator sport because it breeds intolerance. When you write with your students and give them a chance to review and to comment on what you've written, you learn to respect their feelings as writers and you show respect for their critical opinions. They in turn will come to feel the same toward you.

6. *You'll learn not to take yourself too seriously.* Some of your writing will be really fine. It will give you a feeling of deep satisfaction and contentment, like sharing with friends a bottle of good wine that you have made yourself. At other times, you'll write drivel. The very keys of the typewriter will seem to turn on you, and everything you write will sound stupid or false.

If you read aloud what you've written during these times, it may sound ridiculous. It may embarrass you or just depress you. This isn't important, however, as long as you're able to admit it. During these dry periods, new ideas are fermenting, and the juices will flow again. Meanwhile, don't allow your temporary cardboard mentality to intimidate you. Your students, as they watch you, will learn that poor writing is only thinking still in process and that we can learn to use it.

7. *Finally, your students will see that you value writing and think it's important*—important enough to do, not just to assign. So important, in fact, that you give class time to drafting and to revising. So important that you are not completing grade books or reading or planning the next lesson while your students are writing. You're writing with them.

WHAT TO DO

There are many ways in which to share writing with students. You don't have to try all of the methods that we will present here. You can do what's comfortable for you. Some people write well with noise and flurry around them, and some people write better tucked away from the world. If you're among the latter, you may find writing in class difficult. (Appreciate that some of your students will feel this way, too!) You can do some writing at home, in this case, and share the results with your students during class. However, they still need sometimes to see you write, even if it's only a few lines at the beginning of class.

Here are a few ideas that various teachers have found work especially well.

1. Begin some class periods with five or ten minutes' worth of freewriting and write with students. Seat yourself at your desk and be writing as the students come in. Put a note on the blackboard asking students to join you and to keep the noise down. Your message to them is that they are writers, and, as writers, they share responsibility for creating a workshop atmosphere in which good writing can take place.

2. Keep a journal. On some days you may not have much to say. Then you can write about how hard it is to write when you have nothing to say. On other days ideas will pile up right on top of one another. As a journal keeper, you earn the right to call yourself a writer, published or not. Do as the author of the following excerpts does, and share your journal entries aloud with your students.

May 18, 198—

Bad day. Students didn't get objectives of lesson. Why? This bothered me after working all weekend to make it clear. Am I angry at them or myself?

May 18, 198—

We spent time writing out objectives – "The objectives of this lesson were..." I'm amazed at the answers. Some are exactly right – they've read my mind. This is encouraging. They understand *more than I thought. Best part was hearing everyone read aloud. Kids are shocked — sometimes amused — to hear what other kids think. Some can't believe anybody has the same thoughts they do. Surprise — learned more listening to the kids who <u>missed</u> the point of the lesson totally than from listening to the ones who got it.*

3. Try to get something published. Whether you succeed is really secondary. (Though getting that first check, however small, is still a kick.) What's important is that you keep trying. When you're wondering what to do on Monday, you can talk to students about the pitfalls of trying to get something published and about how rotten it feels to wait for weeks and get another one of those impersonal rejection slips in the mail (Figure 6.1).

4. Devote some class time to writing and to revising. In this way your students will have a chance to ask you questions about their work, and you can ask them some. Seek their advice often, and you'll learn from each other. This whole opportunity will be missed if you always write at home.

5. Share both your writing and your feelings about the writing with your students. If something seems to help, tell them about it. What's your secret? When the next line just won't come, do you raid the

November 29, 1982

Thank you for giving us the opportunity to consider the enclosed material. It has been read by members of the staff, and we are sorry that it is unsuited to our present needs. We regret, too, that the large amount of material we receive makes it impossible for us to offer individual comment.

The Editors

V. L. Penman
P.O. Box 1013
Beaverton, Oregon 97075

Dear V. L. Penman:

Thank you for sending us MARVIN, ARE YOU LISTENING? to consider for publication. Several of us have read it, and while some aspects of your story appealed to us, we feel it is not right for our list.

We appreciate your letting us see this, and we would be glad to see more of your work. MARVIN, ARE YOU LISTENING? is returned herewith, most regretfully.

Yours sincerely,

Editorial Department

refrigerator; read your mail; go out for fresh air; listen to music; or do some aerobic dancing? Talk to yourself? Share, share. Your idea might help somebody else.

What problems do you have? What really bugs you? Do you ever read over what you have just written and hate it? Do you ever read something to yourself and think, "pretty good" and then read it to someone else who just sits there and stares at you in sympathy? This can hurt, but it helps to know that somebody else has had the same unpleasant experience. Encourage students to "tell the stories" of their writing experiences, orally or in writing, and to share them with the group. Tell yours, too. This process of writing and sharing yields ideas from which writers in the group will benefit, and—equally important —it builds camaraderie.

6. Sometimes, write impromptu on the blackboard. This is scary the first time or two. You can do it, though.

Tell your students, "OK, you can think up any topic you want, and we'll work on it together. I'll start developing some ideas on the blackboard, and then I'll write up here, in front of you. You can work at the privacy of your own desks." You'll find it isn't always easy to work with someone else's topic, but by watching you the students will learn some strategies for taking a broad, general topic and personalizing it by relating it to their own experience. They'll also have a chance to see what a first draft looks like as it is pouring out of someone else's head. Don't worry that it won't be great or that you'll make lots of false starts; so much the better. They're doing this, too. If you write something you don't like, cross it out. Don't erase everything; have the nerve to leave it up there, crossed out. This is what revision looks like. If it's messy, it has soul. It's writing in the *becoming* phase.

7. Work with your students in developing criteria that you'll use together to judge quality writing: yours, theirs, and others'. Read lots of writing samples aloud, and ask students to identify the qualities that make the good ones work and the characteristics that flaw the others. Out of this rudimentary beginning, gradually, you can develop your own scoring guide—a set of criteria that belong to you, that reflect your values as a community of writers, and that provide the basis for analyzing and revising your own work. You'll also help your students to develop a writer's ear.

You should write too, under the same conditions—on the board or in your notebook—and share your writing first. It's a matter of ethics. You are going to be seeing their work; it's only fair that they see yours (Murray, 1985, 76).

■ SCENARIO

Ruth is a high-school teacher. She enters her first-period class carrying a journal.

The students eye her, wondering what's coming. She sits down at her desk and tells them that everyone will be doing some freewriting for the next few minutes. They look at her and then at each other.

Ruth opens her journal and begins to write. Some of the students follow her lead, but others begin whispering to one another.

Ruth scans the room quietly and stands up, walks to the chalkboard, and writes, "Freewriting time. Write with me, please."

The whispering stops. One by one, the students open their notebooks. Some begin writing right away, while others wait a bit to see whether this is really going to continue. Ruth, meanwhile, writes busily. She doesn't interrupt the students or stare at them or walk up and down the aisles. She concentrates on her work. She is still the teacher, but for now, she is also a writer. ■

IF YOU STILL FEEL NERVOUS

In the beginning, nervousness is natural and even valuable. If you found writing simple and fun, how could you have any empathy for your beginning writers? Maybe you're one of those lucky people for whom public exposure holds no terror. Good for you. You can skip this section. However, maybe you're more of a worrier, a person who peeks in your wallet before you get to the checkout counter just to be *absolutely certain* that you have enough money to cover all the groceries. In that case, here are three kinds of worries that no doubt have already occurred to you.

Worry #1: I won't write as well as my students, and this will be embarrassing

Congratulations—you've just come up with the perfect excuse for never writing again after you get out of college. If you didn't get very good grades on your writing then, you reason with yourself, why subject yourself to further torture? If you did get all As and Bs, why press your luck? Maybe some of those teachers who assessed your work then were lazy, busy, tired, or simply didn't know any better. You sneaked by. You know in your heart though that you can't write. If you start putting things on the blackboard, writing on transparencies, reading your work out loud, soon the whole world will be in on your secret, and then what will happen? You'll be back to hiding out, teaching literature.

There are teachers—lots of them—who live in terror of writing in front of anyone, of having anyone see what they write, or of comparing their own work to that of their students. The first thing such teachers should do is to come to grips with the reality that they probably won't be the best writers of our time or even in their school. There probably will be some colleagues who will write better.

Sometimes you'll be lucky enough to get a student with a natural storytelling voice who'll write you right into the ground. This is truly a moment of victory for you, for you helped bring that voice out.

If you don't write brilliantly, will students think you're incompetent? No. Writers have good and bad days, and student writers know this well. They live with this fear all the time. Furthermore, you can afford a few sloppy pieces of writing, can't you? What your students will be judging is not your value as an individual but your effectiveness as a teacher who can use writing—good and bad—to help your students write better.

Worry #2: I'm just too shy to get up there and write in front of anyone

Well, what would you say to a student who told you this? You might say what a teacher once said to one of us: "If you're shy, get rid of it. There's no place for that in my class." I don't think of him with affection, but I do think of him.

You can't will shyness away, of course. (I couldn't anyhow. I fixed a stiff smile on my face that I hoped would fool this tough, demanding teacher, but inside I quailed and quaked.)

Be tolerant of your own shyness. Maybe it's trying to teach you something. Writing, after all, is a highly personal act. You have a right to be scared, but this doesn't give you the right to quit.

Be a little pushy. Shove yourself. If your hand trembles as you lift the chalk to the blackboard, you're taking yourself and your need for success too seriously. Remember this bit of wisdom from Donald Murray: "We don't learn from finished, polished, completed, published writing. We learn from the constructive failures of early drafts" (Murray 1985). You have to fail sometimes to get better. Besides, even when you can't be brilliant, you can be nervy, and this is a kind of success in itself.

Worry #3: I'll write better than my students, and they'll feel intimidated

I was intrigued one day during a workshop when a teacher remarked, "Won't my students feel intimidated, just feel like giving up when they see that I write so much better than they do?" There's self-confidence for you.

Don't worry too much about intimidating students with your competence. After all, you *should* write well—and even better than your students—at least *some* of the time; otherwise, what are you doing up there teaching writing in the first place? What students see when they watch you write well is the benefit that you can give them of your experience and practice. If you've been at it for thirty years longer than they have and you *never* produce anything that gets their blood pumping, they may wonder what all this sweat and sacrifice is about. In any case, students are not likely to feel disappointed if they find out that you're talented. (If you discovered one day that your doctor had never successfully performed surgery, would you feel relieved that she wasn't as intimidating as you'd once thought?)

If you're holding back, fearful of overwhelming your students with your brilliance, you're playing a dangerous game. Now and again, perhaps you will dazzle them, but make no mistake: Keeping ahead of them on a regular basis will take everything you've got to give. Even when you do write well, don't expect cheers and applause: The courage to share will not guarantee you kudos. When the best you've got results in no more response than yawns, sighs, and stares, you may feel like giving up. Don't. Write again. Sharing *is* risky, because what you're sharing is not the text—not really—but yourself. When it does not work, it is natural for you to feel rejection, but when it does work, the sense of rapport is satisfying indeed.

■ SCENARIO

Burt is a high-school teacher who has been writing with his tenth-grade students for most of the school year. It's now March. Writing with his students has caused him to make some changes in the way he teaches writing, as he admits to a fellow teacher, Charlie.

"Some of those assignments I used to hand out were real turkeys, but I didn't know it till I tried writing on the same thing. My writing was awful—worse than I like to admit. In the beginning of the year, before anybody knew anybody else's handwriting, I put a few papers on the overhead anonymously. I stuck mine up there, figuring they'd recognize it right off and be afraid to comment for fear of offending me. I didn't have to worry. Mine blended right in. But now, after writing for a few months, I'm sounding less like a computer, and, besides, I think my *teaching* is improving. I'm learning to listen to the students.

"I wrote this piece about a month ago about my visit to Washington, D.C. I thought I should show them that a teacher, an educated person like me, would be extremely 'sensitive' to my surroundings, would really notice things, and would get a lot more out of it than just the average jerk on the street. Do you know what this one student said to me? 'It sounds like you're writing to your mother.'

"She was right—I *was* writing a phoney travel brochure. So I redid it, telling them how I really felt—that the tour guides were boring, my feet got too hot, the bus smelled terrible, the hotel was noisy, the cheese hors d'oeuvres made me sick, and so on. It still wasn't great, but at least I wasn't writing to my mother. I was writing for them *and* for me, and I was telling the truth." ■

MAKING IT WORK

You can foul up your writing (a lot) and still make a success of writing with your students. You can jumble clauses and be wordy. You can put your introduction where you thought the conclusion should go. You can tack on a corny title or write bad dialogue. All of these things and more your students will forgive, but the one thing they will not forgive is phoniness.

Be sure you write from the heart. You'll pay for it if you don't. For a real experience in terror, just try getting up in front of a group of students to read something you don't mean. In the eyes of your audience you'll read the two responses every writer dreads most: indifference and distrust.

Meaning what you say isn't so hard once you've learned to write for yourself as the first audience. When we tell student writers to "write for an audience," we usually mean "write for us." We don't mean "write for yourself—*enjoy* what you write." We should, though, because until you can write for yourself and like what you have to say, you can't really write for anybody else. Ask your student writers whether they like what they write, and you'll discover that many don't even know how to answer this question. Yet liking what you write is one of the first steps toward developing a true writer's voice.

When should you start writing with your students: next week; next term; next year; as soon as you take that seminar to brush up? No. Begin now—right now. Write something tonight at home. Write tomorrow in class and as often as you can after that—every day, if possible. Make writing a part of who you are. While you're at it, don't write to your mother, your principal, or that teacher who used to stand over you with the red pen. Write for you. Write from your heart, and you'll want to read it tomorrow, next week, and a year from now. Your students will want to read it, too.

7

DEVELOPMENT OF CRITERIA

- I used to idle Michelle.
- I don't even have lunch because I like her so much.
- She had short brownish blonde hair and her bangs hung over her eyes, which were a bright yellow color from when she had dyed them.
- Debbie is a good sport. She never gives up even if she gets hit in the head by a ball and looks like she is going to drop dead.
- One day, in liticher. . . .
- When I am with him, my heart bellows for love.
- The blonde was found dead with stab wounds in the Bronx.
- I had a crush on her until I found out she was a teacher, then I forgot about her.
- I think if God never made boys there would not be any spunk in her flexible bones.
- She lives at the resistance of Ron and Beverly.
- I hope your happy now that I've written this because I've got a cramp in my arm.
- I think wars should be like they use to be — just guns, tanks, stuff like that.
- Living is a life-long experience.

> ■ *I have decided on youth and Asia for when I can't do anything fun anymore.*
> ■ *The main reason I value life is death.*

Good evaluation of writing demands explicit, written criteria. Until criteria are written down, they're still nebulous: You can't quite get hold of them; they're elusive and a little dangerous. They can be misused. Evaluators who work from criteria that exist only in their heads are quite free to make the most whimsical, impulsive judgments and to persuade everyone, including themselves, that their conclusions are both logical and defensible. Maybe they are, but what if they are not?

WHERE THE CRITERIA COME FROM

In this book, we present readers with a set of criteria for good writing that are well defined and that have been used by hundreds of teachers to score thousands of student writing samples, from kindergarten through college level (and some professional adult writing, as well). These criteria have been tried and tested, and the teachers who have worked with this scoring guide have liked it, for the most part. This is hardly surprising, since the guide was developed *by* teachers *for* teachers; it was not handed down by evaluators who thought that these were the criteria that teachers ought to look at. Rather, these criteria represent the things teachers themselves (at many levels) said that they felt were important in student writing.

This doesn't mean, however, that this is the only analytical scoring guide you should use or even that it's the best guide. You need to ask yourself what it is *you* value in writing and then ask to what extent those values (together with the values of your students) are reflected in this scoring guide. The scoring guide in this book is itself a text in evolution, a reflection of some persons' current thinking about what makes writing succeed. Two years from now—or five or ten—it might look different as we continue to think and to learn.

One of the serious criticisms of analytical scoring has been that language arts teachers cannot agree on what is important in students' writing, and, thus, no workable scoring guide can be developed. This is nonsense. When we introduce the analytical scoring approach in workshops, we sometimes ask teachers to identify the traits that they consider to be the most important ones in writing—not just in student writing but any writing (for example, if you were to browse in your local bookstore in search of something worth reading, what things would you look for?).

Virtually every list that has been generated in every writing workshop covers the traits that are mentioned in the analytical scoring guide presented in this book. The language may be slightly different: for example, some people refer to "voice" as "style"; some people say that a piece needs "unity and cohesiveness" instead of "organization," that "it should start somewhere and go somewhere," or that "it should have a beginning, middle, and end." However, these are semantic differences and not philosophical gaps. In truth, language arts teachers do agree, with remarkable consistency, about what is important in writing. This consistency tells us that the power for developing good criteria is well within the reach of any group of teachers. They have only to make time to talk about writing and be willing to get those criteria out of their heads and onto paper.

SHOULD YOU START OVER?

Suppose you use the analytical scoring guide presented in this book and discover that it works very well for you. Other teachers understand it; you get high interrater agreement in district assessment, and the guide makes sense to the students. Is there any good reason to start fresh with your own scoring guide? The answer is yes, but it's not essential, of course.

You should realize that as with any writing, it's the process of development itself that has the most value; it isn't just the product but also the guide that counts. So, even if you want to use the analytical scoring guide with your students, there is still a good reason to let them explore writing for themselves and to come up with their own list of criteria for judging writing. Students are often a great deal more open to assessment and evaluation when they have a chance to help establish the rules. In putting together their own analytical scoring guide, they'll learn far more about the dos and don'ts of writing than they'll usually learn from complying with somebody else's rules, however well written they may be.

HOW TO DEVELOP AN ANALYTICAL SCORING GUIDE

Let's say that you want to develop an analytical scoring guide for use in your own classroom. Here are five steps that will allow you to do this. As we describe these steps and elaborate on them in this chapter, we will focus on the value of helping students become evaluators of their own and each others' work. This is a very effective way to *teach* writing.

Bear in mind, however, that these same steps can be carried out by *teachers* also, so you may choose to use this approach in the classroom with students. Or you may choose to use it with colleagues as a way of making your evaluation strategies more consistent or as a way of comparing your method of approaching writing with theirs. Here, then, are the five steps.

1. First, do some brainstorming with your students (or colleagues). Find out what they think is important in a piece of writing. Write their responses on the blackboard and leave them up throughout the session to help generate new ideas.

Spelling Ideas Thoughtful Surprises... good title Natural-sounding Liveliness cohesiveness logic Details, details! memorable teaches the reader Spontaneity Goes somewhere readable Makes sense Imagery — I can picture it! GOOD ENDING Vivid Good dialogue moves along Fun to read HUMOR Makes me think! Strong sentences Interesting characters gets me involved right away.

2. Next, give students some writing samples to rank and to analyze. Your collection need not be elaborate. Choose, say, four to six papers, all of which have been written on the same topic, all from the same grade level, and preferably not from the class that is developing the criteria. (It's easier to be objective about someone else's writing.) Ask the students to rank the papers in order, from the highest in overall quality to lowest in overall quality and then to write down their reasons for their choices. They should write about what they like in the papers, as well as what they do not like.

3. Ask the students to meet in small groups of three or four to compare notes, possibly to rerank some papers, and to refine, expand, or revise their written responses. At the end of this session, each student group should have a rudimentary list of traits or qualities that they feel are important.

4. Put each group's list on the blackboard. Make comparisons. See

where there are overlaps. After some discussion, see if you can do some condensing to narrow the total list to five or six "most important" traits.

5. Assign just *one* trait to each small group and ask them to identify the *strengths* and *weaknesses* for that trait, based on *what they actually see* in the writing samples. It is vital that criteria come out of their immediate responses to the writing in front of them and not from memory or hypothesis or from what they feel would be "the right thing to look for."

At this point, you have a checklist of strengths and weaknesses relative to each trait in your scoring guide. Make it clear that this list of criteria can (and should) change over time as students learn more about what makes writing work. Also, it's quite possible to have a separate checklist for special-purpose writing, for instance, a science research paper.

Pages 153 to 155 show a simple checklist to show you how yours *might* look. A checklist like this can be used effectively in peer review or for students' independent revision. Remember, this is just an illustration. Your students can invent one that is just as good as this one, if not better.

WHAT STUDENTS GAIN

From this process of developing your own analytical scoring guide, your students (or colleagues) gain a sense of ownership about the criteria used in the classroom to judge writing. Now their own values are reflected in responsible classroom assessment.

It's understood by both teachers and students that responses to writing, whether expressed as scores, grades, or comments, will be defensible or supported by agreed-upon criteria that reflect the thinking of the writers who employ those criteria. Furthermore, students who know how to assess writing do not have to wait for a teacher's response to know whether what they have written works; they can make this judgment for themselves.

Because the traits and criteria can be used in reviewing both published literature and the students' own work, there is an implicit suggestion that all writers form a community, share some common goals, suffer some common difficulties, and have the same need to reach out to readers. Some student writers may never write a novel or a short story or may never write anything for which they'll receive a paycheck, but they will begin to think of themselves as writers and not simply as observers of writing.

Furthermore, as students build and refine their own criteria for judging writing, they must pay attention to what they're really seeing in that writing. They must think. This process ultimately is more important than learning to score analytically, and scoring is an ideal tool for encouraging thinking about writing.

If children are to make reading-writing connections, they need both to see themselves as authors and to see the authors behind their reading. This is so obvious it is easy to overlook (Calkins, 1986, 229).

WRITING CHECKLIST

TRAIT 1: IDEAS AND CONTENT*

Strengths	*Weaknesses*
_____ Interesting	_____ Lacking in purpose or theme
_____ Well focused	_____ Rambling
_____ Clear	_____ Unclear, muddled
_____ Detailed, complete, rich	_____ Broad, general, vague
_____ Written from experience	_____ Not believable
	_____ Boring

TRAIT 2: ORGANIZATION

Strengths	*Weaknesses*
_____ Good introduction	_____ Details seem out of place
_____ Good placement of details	_____ Introduction boring, predictable
_____ Strong transitions	_____ Transitions absent, weak, or too obvious
_____ Smooth, easy pace	_____ Doesn't go anywhere
_____ Reader doesn't have to think about organization	_____ Wanders aimlessly
_____ Strong conclusion	_____ Stops abruptly
_____ Starts somewhere: goes somewhere	_____ Drags on too long
_____ Builds in tension: creates interest	_____ Bogs down in trivia

TRAIT 3: VOICE

Strengths	*Weaknesses*
_____ Individual	_____ Trite
_____ Honest	_____ Flat

*For the sake of consistency, we've based our checklist on the same six analytical traits that were used in the scoring guide; however, your list of traits might be quite different.

_____ Natural	_____ Writer sounds bored
_____ Expressive	_____ Phoney
_____ Unusual, unexpected	_____ Written to please others
_____ Appealing	_____ Blends with others
_____ Written to be read and enjoyed	_____ Mechanical, lifeless

TRAIT 4: WORD CHOICE

Strengths	*Weaknesses*
_____ Precise language	_____ Language vague, abstract
_____ Strong verbs	_____ Mostly *is, are* verbs
_____ Specific, concrete nouns	_____ Hard for reader to picture anything
_____ Natural	_____ Redundancy
_____ Words used in new way	_____ Too many clichés
_____ Strong imagery	_____ Words used incorrectly
	_____ Words used to impress

TRAIT 5: SENTENCE FLUENCY

Strengths	*Weaknesses*
_____ Fluid	_____ Awkward
_____ Musical, poetic in sound	_____ Jarring word patterns
_____ Easy to read aloud	_____ Hard to read aloud
_____ Interesting word patterns	_____ Short, choppy sentences
_____ Good phrasing	_____ Long, rambling sentences
_____ Varied sentence length	_____ Repetitious patterns
_____ Varied sentence structure	_____ Fragments awkward (sound accidental, tacked on)
_____ Varied sentence beginnings	
_____ Fragments used well	

TRAIT 6: CONVENTIONS

Strengths	*Weaknesses*
_____ Correct or phonetic spelling	_____ Spelling faulty, not phonetic
_____ Punctuation works with sentence structure	_____ Punctuation doesn't work well with sentence structure
_____ Some sophisticated punctuation attempted	_____ Grammatical problems
_____ Correct grammar	_____ Faulty usage
_____ Sound usage	_____ Lack of subject-verb agreement
_____ Paragraphing enhances organization	_____ No paragraphing
_____ Informalities in punctuation or usage handled well	_____ Paragraphs start at wrong spots
_____ Attention to details (i.e., dotted i's, crossed t's)	_____ Careless, hasty errors
	_____ No title
_____ Effective title	_____ Misleading title
_____ Good margins	_____ No margins
_____ Easy to read	_____ Hard to read

STUDENTS AS RATERS OF PAPERS

What is the toughest thing for student writers to acquire and the single thing most needed by a writer in revising his or her own work? Perspective. The reason raters in a formal district or state assessment get so good at evaluating student writing is that they see thousands upon thousands of student papers in a short period of time. They have a chance to see how different writers choose to deal with a common topic, and from that comparison emerges invaluable insight about what does or does not work.

Terms like "coherent" and even "specific" are notoriously hard for students to grasp because they do not read stacks of student writing (perspective) (Elbow, 1987, 154).

Student writers, by contrast, often see only what they've written themselves. Some may never even go back to read that with care. If they're lucky, they might see or hear a few other papers in the context of peer review, but this is not enough to give them a true perspective.

When a student hears only one other text that sounds very similar to his or her own, it may not occur to that student to question the originality of the thinking. Instead, the student writer may take comfort in the thought that he or she probably did it right, since someone else said the very same thing. The writer doesn't see yet that sameness reduces ideas and makes them impersonal and uninteresting.

When we're constantly immersed in our own writing, it's impossible to step back and be objective. Because writing is a solitary and often frightening act, we tend to cling too tightly to the words of others for support. Finding and trusting one's own voice takes time. Students need to see and hear what many other students have written. Only then can they begin to appreciate the strength of diversity, which enriches and enlarges each idea. In any group of papers, only those with voice, those in which the writer speaks the truth, will command the listeners' and readers' attention.

CAN STUDENTS LEARN TO SCORE PAPERS?

Many teachers are teaching their students to score papers analytically as part of writing instruction. You can too. Here's a systematic way of going about it, and you can use these procedures with students from grades 4 and up (you may be able to use it at lower grade levels; you will have to judge your students' readiness for yourself).

1. *Determine which analytical scoring guide you will use.* You may want to use an analytical scoring guide that you and your students have developed together, according to the procedures described earlier, or you may want to use one that has been presented in this book. You can also use a checklist like the one on pages 99-100 or the one on pages 153-155. Whichever guide you use, print enough copies so that every student can have one. Some teachers also find it useful to post an enlarged copy of the scoring guide, or at least a list of the traits, where the students can read it all the time.

2. *Work with the traits one at a time.* Let students see and talk about the full range of traits, but when you first begin scoring, score one trait only and let the students build some confidence in working with that trait before you add others. For example, if you're using the analytical scoring guide from this book, you might begin with voice first (because students will invariably respond to this trait as readers and listeners) and ask students to score papers for this trait only. Then you can go on to ideas and content, organization, word choice, sentence fluency, and, finally, conventions.

As you introduce each trait, *model* the strengths and weaknesses you want students to look for by reading sample papers aloud. Do not, incidentally, just pass out papers for students to read; this is not the same thing. When you read a paper aloud, you help make that paper more the same for each reader/listener than it would be if each student read it individually and silently. Further, you help build students' listening skills.

Obviously, reading aloud imposes its own interpretation on a text. If you're reading something you don't like, you can make it sound dry and dreadful. Similarly, you can inject humor, grace, and style into what you like. As your students gain skill, therefore, you'll want *them* to begin reading aloud, so that more than one voice can be heard. You may even want to hear how a single text sounds through many different voices. In the beginning, however, you need to model this process. Also, you need to acquaint students with the importance of *hearing*, not just seeing, the text.

3. *Talk about the traits as you analyze literature, not only when you are teaching writing specifically.* As you discuss a story, an essay, or a book that you're reading, talk about its effectiveness as a piece of writing: Is the voice strong? Why? Does the introduction work well? How are ideas developed? Does it bog down in places? Are certain spots dull? Is it believable? Do you think the writer knows what he or she is talking about? What words or phrases do you like or dislike?

4. *Talk about the fact that no analytical scoring guide will fit every piece of writing like a glove and that students will have to make "guesses" sometimes in scoring papers.* Stress the fact that the scores per se are less important than the rationale underlying each judgment. Students should be prepared to defend their scores, based on the criteria and on what they actually see in the writing. The scores are just a vehicle for promoting discussion about writing. It's the discussion itself that counts. Students learn about writing by talking about it.

5. *Ask students to assign scores sometimes individually and at other times in pairs or groups.* After students have scored individually, let them discuss their scores in pairs or small groups first and *then* in a large group. Tell them that they can change their minds after the discussion if they then see things differently. Ask for a show of hands ("How many gave this a 5 on organization?") and tally the results on the blackboard where everyone can see them (see Figure 7.1).

	5	4	3	2	1
SCORES					
Ideas	3	17	4	1	—
Organization	2	18	5	—	—
Voice	5	20	—	—	—
Word Choice	—	—	4	16	5
Sentence Fluency	—	1	21	3	—
Conventions	5	3	6	10	1

FIGURE 7.1. Scoring Grid

6. *Discuss any discrepancies that occur.* Don't expect too much agreement on the scores at first. If students disagree, this is generally a plus, because it helps them to start talking. Through their comments they will teach each other about what makes writing work. Allow some time for personal responses ("I didn't like it" or "It made me angry") but also ask them to give reasons for their scores, based on the criteria that you've set for yourselves as a writing group. Ask them to point to specific places in the text where they see evidence of good or weak organization, word choice, and so forth.

It's usually easier to find fault than to identify strengths, and it's also more refreshing to end on a positive note. Let's assume you're using a 5-point scale, which we've used with the analytical scoring guide in this book. Ask students who have assigned 1s and 2s to explain the reasons behind the scores they've given first. Then give the floor to the 4s and 5s.

Continue the discussion until everyone who wishes has had a chance to speak; then revote. Often, several students will change their scores at this point. However, if they don't, don't be too concerned. As you probably realize by now, precision in scoring is not what the process is all about. It is the discussion of the scores and of the responses to the writing that matters most. However, the fact remains that given good criteria and time to practice scoring, raters (whether they're teachers or students) will agree very closely (within a point) in their responses a remarkable percentage of the time.

Some writing, however, seems to defy such agreement. Here's where evaluation purists get uncomfortable. "Come on now," they say, "if your system is worth anything, you should be able to get trained raters to agree on *any* piece of writing." This is not necessarily true. (We are not measuring temperature or pH factor.) If we are honest about it, we must admit that much of how we respond to any text comes out of what we bring to it. No text is *precisely* the same for any two readers, and it will not stay constant over time. The *Huckleberry Finn* that you read at age twelve is not the same book that you may read at age thirty. Or at age sixty. The words on the pages are the same, but the meaning that you give the words you read changes always. To deny this is to deny literature its power. Some text is simple. It's functional writing: "Gone to the store for avocados. Back at 5." There is no need to muse over meaning here. Where the text is rich and complex, it invites multiple responses. The truth about any piece of complex writing is bigger than any score or set of scores will allow us to express, and this is as it should be.

7. *Periodically review and reflect on your criteria.* If lots of discrepancies occur with virtually every paper, the fault may lie with the scoring guide itself, rather than with the way the students are applying it.

Review your criteria and ask yourself the following questions.

Are the criteria very specific, or is some of the language vague?

Is the language understandable to the students? Have you avoided terms that have no meaning to some readers? Have you discussed words and phrases that puzzle students?

Is the language in the scoring guide a good match with what readers actually find in the writing, or does it just look good on paper?

Is there a real difference, as you've defined it, between a 5 paper and a 3; between a 3 paper and a 1?

8. *Let students score some of your own writing.* Do you have a sample paper that you wrote in grade school, junior high school, or even high school? Give your students a chance to rate it but don't tell them it's yours. Here's one that I've used in workshops with teachers from time to time:

> Here I am in Williston! I can hardly believe it! Darlene about dropped her teeth when I came sailing in. Tonite I am going to see Radar, the world's best horse, and then to a shower for Vicki Gordon, a life guard at the pool.

"What kind of person wrote this?" I ask the workshop participants. "Shallow," they tell me, "timid," "self-conscious," "a real goody-goody."

"How old is this person?" I ask them. "Twenty," "twelve," "fourteen." Fourteen is about right. When I tell them the paper is mine, we share a good laugh. Writers become pretty thick-skinned, especially about old stuff. Sometimes, when the students find out that it's mine, they will point out how it really *does* have voice after all. I assure them it's a 3, and this is probably generous, but I'm not always so gushy and breathless now, so there's hope.

9. *Score some samples from textbooks.* Don't be surprised to find that samples from textbooks score much higher on conventions and sentence structure than on ideas or voice. In our fervor to make textbooks "readable" over the past few years, we've pretty well squashed the voice right out of them. Heaven forbid students should use some of these texts as models of fine writing. They will, though, unless we give them freedom to teach themselves otherwise.

On another level, the textbooks themselves were poor models of writing and thinking within the disciplines they represented. . . . They were dull and gave little sense of the organizing concepts that might matter within the discipline (Langer and Applebee, 1987, 147).

Pull some excerpts from the newspaper and from magazines too. Let your students bring in samples. Try pulling some pieces from published (and famous) writers but handwrite the copy so that students do not recognize it immediately as a published piece. The scores will often surprise you and your students. Also try *typing* some samples of your students' writing. Again, the scores may surprise you.

Finally, don't forget to revise your analytical scoring guide as your students gain new ideas about what makes writing work.

■ SCENARIO*

Eric, a sixth-grader who was fond of eagles, had written a story about freedom and captivity with a bit of a twist. He hoped his teacher would like it, but there was one big problem. The paper was two days late. Would this matter much? He handed it in, hoping for the best. Here is Eric's paper, exactly as he wrote it.

In disgust, my friend and I soared over a huge city that had been a vast land where our ancestors once roamed. We were heading to our winter refuge in a remote mountain area of Alaska. All of a sudden, we hear a loud CRACK! The next thing I knew, a flying net had caught my friend and brought him down.

For awhile I hovered over where he fell and observed, but after they put him in their truck, that was it! I swooped down as quickly as I could, but it was too late. The truck started its engine. All I could do was follow it to its destination.

After at least thirty miles I was tired and desperate for food. Luckily, the men in the truck were too. So I dove into a nearby forest and caught two mice, one for me and one for my friend.

When I returned to the truck I said, "Here's a mouse for you because I know you're probably famished."

His reply was, "No. They have plenty of fish in here. But being captured isn't all it's cracked up to be. Please get me out of here!"

Being an eagle, I have a strong beak, but the lock that had been placed on the truck was so incredibly strong, even my beak couldn't break it.

"Well," I said, "the only thing I can do is follow you until they move you to another cage. I must go now. The men are coming. Remember, I will be following you. Good-bye."

"How could they do this to us?" I thought. First they take our land and destroy our trees; then they take us—for what reason, I don't know."

Soon the truck was heading into a city. At this time I had to make a decision whether to risk my life trying to free my friend, or to give up hope and say my last good-byes, hoping that he could get free and find me.

My mind was made up. I had to stay and help him out of captivity.

Later that night the truck stopped at a hotel and I went down to visit my friend. He was weary. All he could say was, "H-E-L-P M-E-E!"

---

*The student writing in this scenario is shared with the permission of Eric Lutz, who is now a ninth-grade student in the Beaverton (OR) School District. Eric was a sixth-grader at the time this story took place.

The next day we were deep in a city. After awhile the truck moved out of the city and then drove up to a park. But when I looked closer, it was more than just a park. It had caged animals.

I decided to investigate, not knowing that the choice I had made would keep me from seeing my friend for two days.

As I swooped down, some people noticed me. They were screaming and I didn't know why. Heck, there was only one of me, and there were over three hundred of them. Frightened, I zoomed over to a tree just out of the boundaries of the park.

After the park closed I went back and got a closer look. To my surprise, I saw an eagle that was enclosed in a cage. Sheepishly, I said, "Hel-hello."

"Ahh," he replied, "someone of my own kind."

"What is this place?" I asked. "Why do you want to live in cages, and why do humans stare at you?"

"Well," he answered, "first of all we don't have a choice. Humans caught us and put us here, and other humans stare at us in awe. Don't you see, you're in a zoo?!"

"My friend has been captured. Is there any hope of getting him out?" I asked.

"Well," he replied, "there is only one way. It's risky, but with your help it just might work."

"How?" I asked.

"At feeding time the feeder has to open the cage to get the food in. If you attack him after he opens the door, you and your friend will be free," he answered.

The next night they put my friend in a cage and he and I went over the plan. At feeding time the next day the feeder opened the door to the cage, and I swooped down and hit him. Once again the crowd was screaming.

"Get out!" I screeched as my friend dashed out.

We were free again.

When the papers were handed back, Eric held his breath. Had she liked it? Was it a good idea, pretending to actually *be* the eagle, or had she found it too corny? The questions most pressing in Eric's mind were not answered. There was only a letter grade and one short comment, written at the top of the page: "D (2 days late)." Eric's heart sank. It wasn't the grade so much, although that was bad enough, but what about his idea; what about the words and phrases he'd struggled over, changed, and smoothed out? She hadn't noticed, apparently.

"I hate writing," he told his mother. "Nobody likes what I write anyway."

Eric's mother, who is a teacher, took Eric's paper to a colleague, whose sixth-graders were learning to score one another's writing analytically, and asked for their responses. They didn't know about

FIGURE 7.2. Analytical Scores and Comments of Sixth-Grade Class

5	Ideas/Content
4	Organization
4½ ~~5~~	Voice
~~4~~ 5	Word Choice
4½	Sentence Structure
5	Conventions

I liked the ending the best. The plan was a good idea. It has very good suspence and detail. But I can't say how much I liked it in words but it was EXELLENT!

P.S. The beginning was a little confusing.

5	Ideas/Content
4	Organization
4	Voice
5	Word Choice
5	Sentence Structure
5	Conventions

This is a super paper). It has unusu unusual words and held my attention. However, you could have put a little more on the ending of how the animals got there way through the yor.

5	Ideas/Content
4	Organization
5	Voice
5	Word Choice
4	Sentence Structure
4	Conventions

It was a little confusing in the beginning, I couldn't figure out that they were eagles until the 6th paragraph. Otherwise it was a good idea and written with unordinary words – they weren't boring or the same over and over again. The voice was done well. You could feel that the person was talking to you right there.

Eric's story when they scored the paper, and they did not know the grade he'd received. Figure 7.2 shows the analytical scores and comments provided by the sixth-grade students. In addition to the individual responses, the teacher attached to Eric's paper this form, which reflects consensus scores and comments on the total class response:

ANALYTICAL TRAIT
WRITING ASSESSMENT

Rater ID: _____

Analytical Trait			Rating		
1. Ideas and content	1	2	3	4	5
2. Organization	1	2	3	4	5
3. Voice	1	2	3	4	5
4. Word Choice	1	2	3	4	5
5. Sentence fluency	1	2	3	4	5
6. Conventions	1	2	3	4	5

Comments:
Hope this is helpful. Thank you for sharing, Eric—our class enjoyed your writing. Please send more. Kids were confused as to what animal; they felt that info was too late.

Eric was delighted by the range of responses from an audience of students his own age. They were honest, specific, and based on the writing itself, nothing else. "I feel like a writer now," was how he summed it up. "I'm going to keep these forever."

The sixth-graders who scored Eric's paper were just beginning to work with analytical scoring. Eric's paper represented only their second attempt to score all six traits. Yet, obviously they were already getting a good feeling for what each trait meant and they seem confident and comfortable in their analysis.

What about the teacher's grade of D? It didn't carry much of its original sting after the very positive feedback Eric received from his peers. This is probably just as well, for this grade seems to have been based (at least partly) on punctuality and not writing performance. We need to be extraordinarily clear about what it is we're responding to. If it's work habits, let's say so: "It simply infuriates me when you do not turn your work in on time." Using grades to deliver emotional messages or to punish students is dishonest.   ■

STUDENT RATERS AND GRADING

Sometimes teachers ask whether students' scores should be considered in assigning grades. Our feeling is that students should not score or grade one another's work in any formal sense and that student-assigned scores should not be recorded or used in grading. They can, however, be shared with student writers. The independently derived responses of peers (often very different from the group response obtained through peer review) offers valuable feedback. If nothing else, it's useful to find out that not everybody will react to your writing in the same way. Grading, however, must still remain the teacher's responsibility.

It is also useful for students to score their own work and to compare their scores to what a teacher assigns. The teacher's judgment should be the final one, but there should always be opportunity for students to question and to discuss. Teachers can get busy and tired. They can overlook things, sometimes they skim papers, and now and again miss the point. When students question their grades, they may be only disappointed, or complaining, or just simply wrong. If the writing doesn't work, no amount of regret or compassionate open-mindedness will make it work. Sympathy scores and grades make teachers feel guilty and students suspicious. On the other hand, it's a poor teacher who cannot change his or her mind about a piece of writing and say, "Well, yes, now that I read it again, I see it quite differently." Students should feel that there's hope to change a teacher's mind, but they should also understand that they'll have to present a convincing case.

A FINAL COMMENT

Teaching analytical assessment requires restraint. If you jump in every few seconds to clarify or to insert your own definitions, you'll teach students to rely on your opinions instead of working toward their own understanding of the traits. Resist the temptation to hand too much to the students; make them work for it instead.

Over time—and it takes some time—students learn to listen to each other (for the most part) and to integrate the thinking of others with their own. The first time they have a discussion based on analytical scoring, this probably won't happen. Maybe they won't say much, or, if they do talk, each will have his or her own message to deliver. This is fine. Be patient. Encourage students to be opinionated. Let them know, however, that the capacity to change one's mind, based on persuasive evidence, is a strength. If someone has a different opinion, they ought to be asking why. Maybe that one dissenting reader sees something in the text the others have missed.

■ SCENARIO

Peggy, a seventh-grade teacher, has taught her students to score writing analytically. They are working on voice and are defining it as they score by listening to what *each* reader finds in a paper.

Todd, who has been a reluctant writer all year, raises his hand eagerly for the first time in a long while, and Peggy goes to his desk.

"This is me—exactly," he tells her, pointing a finger at the criteria in the scoring guide that define voice at the 3 level. "This is me. I'm a 3 in voice."

For a moment, she isn't sure how to respond.

"I know what to do about it, though," he tells her joyfully. "I'm going to stop writing for you. I'm going to write for me." ■

8

TEACHERS WITH TEACHERS

- Space is a place where lots of people don't go very often.
- The happiest day of my life was 1979.
- I can't really say I have had the happiest day of my life yet. Either it hasn't happened or I just can't remember.
- It takes many years and lots of fights to get a good friend.
- We said the Pledge of Elegance.
- My truck is like a little brother to me.
- There we were, talking face to face and ear to ear.
- Being alive helps give one a more positive outlook.
- Life is the symptom of the universe, but yet the cure of the galaxy.
- Those years stuck in my mind like flies to paper.
- We were inspired by Mary Lou Rettons great performance on the volt.
- Because Egypt was a third-world country, we couldn't just go out and get a hamburger anytime we felt like it.
- Maybe we're gifted because we hardly ever fight like some people.
- He sure is smart despite how tall he is.
- She was most generally nice to everyone, unless they had done her wrong.

Teachers who work with other teachers in reviewing, discussing, and assessing students' writing give themselves permission to think openly about what good writing is and how to teach it effectively. They give themselves permission to change their minds as they learn. Intellectually and psychologically, teachers need this time with one another. They need to hear what other teachers think and to share experiences with the experts: themselves. How can you provide this time?

One way is to form a group that meets regularly to write, to read, to score papers, and to talk about student writing and other literature. This teachers-with-teachers concept is important, not so much because it keeps assessment alive (assessment must never be seen as an end in itself) but because it keeps the spotlight on the importance of *writing* and encourages teachers to continue thinking that there is always a new way to look at what we think we know. We learn to write forever. We learn to teach writing forever.

A teachers' writing group can

Give writing teachers the time and opportunity they need to talk about writing

Provide a cost-effective, highly valuable inservice opportunity

Become the basis for conducting writing assessment at the building (or even district) level, if that is desired

Provide opportunity for teachers themselves to write and to respond to each others' writing, thereby using writing to learn about teaching and about themselves.

A FLEXIBLE FORUM

The most important thing that happens in a teachers' writing group is that teachers talk to one another about writing and teaching. Of course, they could do this while carpooling, but the impact of the writing group is greater because its whole focus is on writing, and everyone who participates accepts this. These are people who take their craft seriously and want to get better at it.

Teachers' writing groups need not involve every writing teacher within a school, but they work most successfully when everyone gets an invitation and feels wanted. Furthermore, participation need not be limited to the English faculty. Teachers in many disciplines now use writing to teach; they can gain much from participation in a writing group, and they have much to contribute. Teachers of mathematics, psychology, science, social studies, and history who *use* writing to teach have known for years the value of sound ideas, logical organization, and discriminating word choice. Our common philosophical base provides an ideal means to interconnect these disciplines by using writing to build thinking skills in all areas.

Some teachers, of course, avoid using writing to teach other content because they don't want to deal with "correcting" the writing. Who can blame them? Editing belongs in the language arts class. A writing group provides an opportunity to show that there is more to writing than conventional correctness. We cannot show this by talking about it, however. We must do it. We must write, and we must read and hear what others have written.

WHAT A TEACHERS' WRITING GROUP DOES

What the teachers' writing group does in your school might differ from what anybody else is doing, and this is fine, as long as you and your colleagues are benefiting from the experience. Here are a few of the activities that other groups have found to be helpful.

1. *Teachers write and share their own writing with each other.* Through this experience, they improve their own writing skills, get a better grip on revision, learn what it takes to work effectively in a peer support group, create some samples of revised writing to share with students, and abandon some of their apprehensions, or, at least, become realistic about them. Some groups bring in a writer or a consultant to work with them and to run the meetings like a class; others prefer to teach one another in a less formal way.

2. *Teachers share and assess their students' writing.* They may read a few samples aloud, photocopy "problem" papers for everyone in the group to discuss or to score, or (if time permits) bring in a larger sample of papers to be scored as a part of grading. Whatever specific procedure is used, teachers have an opportunity to see how others respond to the writing that their students have done. This is always eye-opening, and usually fun as well. Some teachers coordinate one or more assessments over the year so that all students (from within a building or a grade level) write on the same general topic; this makes comparisons easier.

3. *Groups from two schools exchange and score papers on a regular basis in order to get totally anonymous responses to their students' writing.* This is a good way for small districts to set up a cooperative local writing-assessment group in a way that minimizes costs for both sides.

4. *Teachers share the results of research, based on what they've read, experienced in workshops, or discovered through their own work in the classroom.* Some prefer to use one or more published texts as a focus for the group.

5. *Teachers share and use minilessons as models or strategies that they've tried in class.* They discuss successes and failures, compare notes, and ask what could be done differently next time.

ASSESSMENT LOGISTICS

Let's suppose that your teachers' writing group decides to spend some time assessing students' writing. How would you go about this? Well, your procedures will depend on the purpose of the assessment. Do you want (1) to gain a better understanding of what good writing is or (2) to gather data on your students' performance?

In other words, is the assessment merely a vehicle for examining student writing, or do you want performance data that will tell you something about how your current instructional program is working? These are not conflicting goals, but they are different, and they have a lot to do with how formal and structured you need to be in setting up your building-level assessment. Let's take the case of a formal assessment first and see how this might be set up. Then we'll return to informal assessment.

FORMAL ASSESSMENT: GENERATING PERFORMANCE DATA

Setting up a building-level assessment isn't difficult, but it does take considerable planning time, and it's generally best if one person is in charge of coordinating the effort. That person should, preferably, be someone with experience in assessment. Barring that, look for the person with the best organizational and interpersonal skills.

The logistics of a small-scale formal assessment are similar to those for a large-scale district or state-level assessment. Everything is just a little more low-key. The basic components are the same: You need papers to assess, a comfortable facility in which to conduct the readings, a way of marking and tallying scores, teachers to read the papers, someone to help manage the paper flow and to run errands, and someone to conduct the training, run practice scoring sessions, and oversee the whole process.

Some schools prefer to assess once, either in the fall or in the spring. Fall assessment provides an indication of students' needs, which can then be addressed during the year to come. Spring assessment provides some indication of how students have done over the course of the year, and what their future needs are likely to be. Obviously, however, data from spring assessment are less useful in meeting the instructional needs of the very students from whom that data has been collected.

Some schools like a pre/post format. The pretest, administered sometime in the fall, tells teachers something about their students' current skills. Later, when data are gathered from the post assessment in the spring, teachers can look at differences in performance and draw some cautious conclusions about the impact of their instructional program. (*Cautious,* because chances are that students will be writing on a slightly different topic for the postassessment, a change that in itself can account for some differences in performance.) In addition, very small shifts up or down may or may not be indicative of any real change. People are not machines, and no one writes exactly the same way all the time. However, startling changes in average scores (and sometimes even in individual scores) may be meaningful and are always worth exploring. Often, though (with apologies to statisticians), a close look at the papers themselves tells a more revealing tale than hours of isolated data analysis.

SOME DETAILS TO THINK ABOUT

Remember that every paper you assess must be read twice by raters (teachers) who work independently. The second rater should not know what scores have been assigned by the first rater. Scores can be written on the papers or on separate score sheets, but it's important to have a way of masking the first reader's scores so that the second reader is not influenced.

If you score analytically, each reading will take about two to four minutes, depending on the length of the papers. (Holistic scoring will take slightly less time.) At first, reading may go a little slower than this, but once the teachers get into the swing of it, they can usually go through about fifteen papers (analytically) per fifty-minute reading session. (As we've mentioned, some teachers can score papers much faster than this.)

If raters' scores on any given trait agree within one point, those scores can stand. If they are apart by two points or more, the paper must be read a third time and rescored. The third reading is usually done by the scoring director or by another member of the team. There is, however, some advantage in having raters rescore their own discrepant papers. Taking another look may help teachers to rethink their reasons for scoring papers in a certain way and to ask which score—their own or that of the other rater—is really more defensible.

In most formal assessments, a paper is read by two people who do not know the student at all. Purists will always insist upon this kind of anonymity. At the building level, however, there is some value in having teachers read and score their own papers and then having a second reading done by another teacher. This doesn't mean that only two teachers would see the papers from a particular class, however. On the contrary, it is best if the papers from one class are then divided among all the teachers in the group. In this way, the teachers have the benefit of seeing as many other perspectives as possible and of comparing them to their own. If their own scores are significantly above or below those of the other raters, they cannot then attribute the differences to one person's bias or cranky disposition.

Should all teachers bring papers from all their students? Ideally, yes, but your own answer to this question must depend on the time teachers in your school are willing to devote to reading papers. It is a time-consuming task. It won't seem quite so burdensome, however, if you think of assessment as an in-service activity in which all participants become teachers of one another.

Papers should always be returned to the students. Student writers who participate in an assessment and then receive no feedback feel—rightly—resentful, and the scores alone, apart from the text, mean little. Students need to see their papers again in order to judge the value of the responses.

One last point is needed here. Glancing through the scoring guide and then settling down to score fifty papers is not a good idea. You must allow as much time as you can afford for practice and discussion. Remember that the *real* purpose of good assessment is to provide support for instruction. Nothing profitable is achieved when teachers who are neither prepared nor confident begin assigning numbers whose meaning they're unsure of to papers that they feel they haven't had time to read thoroughly. Time invested early in practice scoring and open discussion of disagreements will be made up later when teachers understand the meanings of the scores that they assign and can interpret these scores verbally to each other, to students, and to themselves.

INFORMAL ASSESSMENT: LEARNING ABOUT HOW STUDENTS WRITE

If your *central* purpose in assessing writing is to learn about the writing itself, as opposed to gathering data, you can be a little more lenient about procedures. However, the raters still need to learn the analytical scoring process so that everyone applies the same criteria in the same way as they assign scores. If some people are still attending more to conventions while others care only for voice, everyone may as well sit home by the fire and read the papers.

Teachers who are new to the analytical scoring process generally require from ten to twenty minutes to team score (in groups of two to four) and to discuss *each* student paper. In a three-hour session (assuming some previous introduction to the analytical scoring process itself has been given), they can team score from six to twelve papers, and everyone leaves the session with a very good sense of what analytical scoring is all about and, generally, with some new insights about writing.

It's often wise to hire a writing-assessment specialist to run a session like this, although a teacher with some experience in analytical assessment can also do it. The most important quality to look for in the person who will be running the scoring session is open-mindedness. Too often, assessment is looked on as a search for the "right" answer, but the truth about a piece of writing, especially one that has some substance to it, is generally very big. There is room for lots of opinions and even contradictions. This is why *precise agreement* on scores is not only difficult to achieve but also *undesirable.* The differences within ourselves cause us to view any piece of writing somewhat differently, and to erase these differences totally makes a sham of assessment. Out of many individual strands we weave a larger truth about any piece of writing, whether it be *Hamlet* or a student essay. The more strands we pull out, the more we weaken the fabric. Thus, insisting that *every* rater view a given paper as a "3 on ideas" or a "4 on voice" is counterproductive.

If all teachers within the school wish to assess all their students, it is usually necessary to set aside a day to complete all the readings. Trying to assess hundreds of papers as an after-school project, especially if it stretches out over several evenings, rarely works well. Teachers are simply too tired. However, if, as some teachers have done, you limit the number of papers assessed each time to, say, twenty or thirty, you may well have a manageable task for an afternoon or, better yet, an early morning session when people are fresh.

Some teachers may prefer to bring only the most difficult papers, those they don't know what to do with, to the session. Others may wish to choose papers at random. Some may wish to bring a cross section from classes at different levels of ability. Any combination is possible as long as teachers do not generalize to the whole student population on the basis of results that may not be representative. We present this caution almost in passing because it's been our experience that the discussion and increased skill in interpreting students' writing is what teachers come to care about, and many soon look on the results as a secondary benefit. Nevertheless, data, once gathered, have a way of taking on a life of their own. This is not to say that writing-assessment data are not of value but only to suggest that from the teacher's perspective, learning to understand what good organization is all about and being able to share this information with student writers is of far greater importance than finding out that the average class score in organization is 3.6.

Over a period of weeks or months, teachers who score papers analytically get faster and more efficient at it. This leaves them with more time for discussing writing or for reading larger numbers of papers, whichever seems more appealing. It also gives them a skill they can use regularly in classroom assessment. Scoring students' writing, they find, is a fast and useful way of providing feedback. There's plenty of time left over, after scoring, to add a personal comment without spending the amount of time that the old line-by-line method required.

Further, only teachers who know the process well will feel comfortable teaching it to students. Others may not even try, and that's a shame. Students with the power and confidence to be their own critics stand a better chance of thinking of themselves as writers.

Some Questions About Assessment

1. *How much training or practice time do teachers need before they begin scoring papers in a formal assessment?* A full day of practice is sufficient for most people to become comfortable with the process. Interrater agreement improves with time, however, as does each teacher's perception and self-confidence. If you are interested in having the most accurate possible data, raters need more than a few hours' worth of practice time before they begin to assign scores that will be used in making important judgments about curriculum or student performance.

Many teachers feel they're "ready" after the first few hours, but inevitably they report that they score differently and feel better about their scores once they've done it for several days. This, of course, has some interesting implications for the way in which grades are usually assigned.

2. *Do teachers' writing groups have to spend large amounts of time scoring papers?* Scoring isn't mandatory. You can simply read and share papers orally, do some writing yourselves, or talk about what other teachers are doing in their classrooms. However, once you start scoring, you may well find that analytical assessment teaches you more about student writing in less time than many other activities. No theoretical text, no matter how persuasive or insightful, can ever teach you as much about student writing as immersing yourself in stacks of student papers with other teachers—the people who work with students every day.

3. *What should you do with writing-assessment results (scores)?* First, here are a couple of things that you should not do. Don't use the results to evaluate teachers, even informally. The information is not broad enough for this, and there are too many extraneous factors affecting students' writing performance (students' attitudes, previous skill levels, nature of the writing prompt, etc.) over which teachers have no control. Don't use results as the *sole* basis for assigning course grades unless you collect multiple results over a long period of time and also look closely at changes in writing performance. Writing-assessment scores are indicators, nothing more.

When a student receives an unusually high score in voice, for example, this doesn't mean that the student has "mastered" the trait of voice and can now go on to other things. Similarly, the student who receives a very low score on one or more traits may simply be having a bad day, may feel disoriented, may not like the topic, or may simply fail to reach the reader who is assigning the score. (Low scores sometimes result from lazy or hasty reading, not inept writing.)

Here then are some things you might do with data.

Keep a record of before and after scores if you do a pre/post assessment. See what the averages tell you about the performance of classes or student groups as a whole. Overall, where do the students' strengths lie? If the strengths are primarily in ideas, organization, and voice, rejoice. This is as it should be. If there are weaknesses in these areas but real strengths demonstrated in sentence structure and conventions, something may be out of joint in the writing process. It could be that too much emphasis is being placed on getting things correct before anything much has been said.

Start a portfolio of each student's writing in order to assess performance over time. A portfolio might contain a sample of the student's work in September and then another sample for each successive month through June. Assessment might look at all traits on all papers or at selected traits on selected papers. Any number of configurations are possible. Clearly, portfolio-based assessment offers a distinct advantage in that it does not rely so heavily on one performance done on one day.

Start a file of photocopied student papers. Look for strong and weak performance examples by trait—for example, strong and weak organization, strong and weak voice. Read these papers aloud to students, and use them as training papers for future assessments, at either the building or the district level.

Interpret scores with one eye on current curriculum. What is receiving the most emphasis in the current curriculum? Considering what happens day to day in the classroom, are the average scores about what you might expect? Where would you most like to see improvements?

Ask yourself what makes particularly strong papers work. Make some notes, and share your thinking with students and with other teachers.

Take time to make some serious comparisons between your perceptions about your students' writing and the perceptions of other teachers who work with you. How do your perceptions differ? What do they see that you have missed? What are you seeing in the papers that they have missed?

■ SCENARIO

Nancy has been teaching writing for six years. Only one year ago she was talking about "burnout," a condition that some colleagues said was just part of the normal fifth-year syndrome.

"This year," she says, "I decided to make the classroom a place I would enjoy coming to. When someone suggested teaching writing as a workshop, though, I really didn't have much faith in it. I thought the kids would be wild. I thought I would hate writing. I thought nobody would learn anything if I didn't give lectures and do drills and give essay tests."

Despite her misgivings, Nancy proceeded with her conviction to do "something different." This year, her classroom is set up as a writing workshop. There are tables and chairs but no desks. "I'm the only teacher here whose classroom looks like this, and it wasn't easy to bring about. My principal didn't like the idea one bit at first."

Even though there are windows all along one wall, Nancy has brought in lamps. Low shelves hold books. Some of the tables are makeshift. Most are donations or cheap leftovers scrounged at garage sales. In one corner, Nancy has set up a reading area with two overstuffed chairs, a rug, lamps, plants, and a library of nonfiction books, some her own, some donated.

In another corner she has set up a reference and editing area that also serves as a small conference area for students. The reference area holds seven different dictionaries and handbooks, a book of synonyms and two thesauruses, books on style and grammar, and a current copy of the *Writer's Market*. A poster on the wall depicts the copyeditor's symbols. There's also a posted list of places that publish student writing. Storage bins hold pens of all types, sharpened pencils, various kinds of paper—plain, lined, and colored. One bin holds several kinds of stationery with envelopes and stamps. There are also felt pens, calligraphy pens, and other artists' tools, together with staplers, paper punches, tape dispensers, paper clips, and other materials.

One corner of the room is reserved for peer group meetings. This area has no tables or chairs. There's a big, well-worn rug on the floor and large pillows scattered around.

When Nancy works with her students, she sits at a small table in the front of the class. There are four chairs at the table so that she can hold individual or group conferences there. The table is low and is pushed to one side of the front so that students have full view of the oversized chalkboard, where Nancy often writes as she's talking with them.

Every day begins with freewriting. Students may write in journals or on scratch paper. Nancy writes with them. Freewriting normally lasts about ten minutes. At the end of this time, Nancy often shares what she's written and invites students to do the same. Students may share as little as one line or even a single word.

Beginning on Tuesdays, more class time is devoted to prewriting and to drafting. Nancy often shares her own story about where she is in the writing process, how far along her text is, what she's done to get it to this point, and what's giving her the most trouble. It might be the introduction. She will model the process she uses to get herself "unstuck" by brainstorming several different introductions on the board, thinking aloud as she goes: "I don't like this one so well. It's draggy . . . spends too much time on description."

Sometimes Nancy will ask the class to write about the process they're going through: "Write what you're thinking *now*. Where are you? What's bothering you? Where will you go next?" They often take time to share these process stories.

Once a week or so, Nancy gives everyone in the class a photocopy of a student paper from the same or a lower grade level. Students are asked to read the paper, to make one positive comment in writing that they think would be helpful to the student writer, and then to score the paper analytically.

"They get to hear what everyone else in the class thinks about the same piece of writing," Nancy explains, "but the price for that is that you have to commit your own opinions first. You have to take a stand and explain the reasons behind your scores; no fair hiding behind 'I just like it.' We do this with some of the literature we read, too."

Nancy reads her own writing aloud to the class and asks them to respond. She often talks about having some writing published, and shares stories of "victories and defeats."

The school has its own publishing house, staffed by Nancy, other writing teachers, and parent volunteers who type students' papers and help bind the materials together. Students contribute artwork, design covers, or otherwise style the published books.

Nancy comments: "Parents are finding out—we're all finding out—that students do have stories to tell. Our job is to draw those stories out. I can't believe how burned out I felt about writing instruction just a year ago. I just couldn't face another sea of bland faces. I couldn't tell if I hated them more for what I thought they were doing to me, or myself more for what I felt I wasn't doing to them.

By literate environment I mean a place where people read, write, and talk about reading and writing; where everybody can be student and teacher; where everybody can come inside (Atwell, 1985, 148).

"Now I look forward to my writing class. It feels good to be here. You can see it on the students' faces. They're writers. They're not coming to class. They're coming to work." ∎

Like Nancy in the preceding scenario, you may have discovered that students—and teachers, for that matter—feel more comfortable and write more productively in a classroom atmosphere that is warm and inviting. Several years ago, we asked a group of high-school writers what things were most important to them in a writing workshop, and here are their answers:

1. I like lots of natural light.
2. Music—soft music—maybe classical.
3. I like a cozy corner to go to sometimes and just read. The corner should have some books: some old and some new—lots of books to read and browse through.

4. Food. Writers get hungry, you know.

5. More writing space. Not such tiny desks. It's better to write at big tables.

6. I like it quiet. Totally quiet.

7. To see outside. To see trees or grass or the sky—something natural.

8. Pictures, posters, lots of colors. Brightness.

9. When I write at home I put slippers on my feet and sit in a rocker and pull a big old quilt over my lap. Can you do that in a writing workshop?

10. My pen is very important to me. I like a good pen that writes smoothly with big, bold lines. Black or blue is OK. I hate pens that skip. I don't write well with a pencil.

11. I like big, clean sheets of white paper. They have to be white. Yellow paper is no good for writing. Sometimes I like to write on stationery.

12. I like to write on posters, wallpaper, old newsprint, paper bags, and such things—things you wouldn't normally think of.

13. There has to be a kind of friendliness in the room. You have to feel welcome.

14. Sitting in a circle is good. Rows are not good for writing.

15. The most important thing for me is knowing there will be somebody there who will want to read what I write (at least some of the time).

SOME PARTING COMMENTS

In numbering the following suggestions, we may have given the impression that they are rules. Please don't look at them in this way. There are no rules in teaching writing, except those that writers make for themselves. There are no magic solutions either, except those that teachers and students come upon together. The following is simply a list of suggestions based on what many teachers have told us works well.

1. Teach students to assess their writing and to develop their thinking as critical readers. Then revision will seem a more natural process.

2. Integrate the teaching of reading and writing. Use discussions of literature not just to talk about meaning, but also to consider what makes a piece of literature worth publishing. Will it speak to more than one generation? Has it already? How? Why?

3. Treat students like writers. Assume for now that the gap between student writers and professional, published writers is primarily a

function of experience. For all we know, this is the case. Sometimes it may also be a function of God-given talent, but we don't know that for sure. At least, not yet. Sometimes talent lies dormant for a long while. And face it: For some professional writers, publication is mostly a matter of luck.

4. Emphasize the positive. This is particularly important in all one-on-one interventions and is also vital at any time that comments are written out. Use a green pen instead of a red one in marking your students' papers. Underline what works well or what you like. Write one specific, positive comment at the end. Save your negative comments, criticisms, corrections, and editorial suggestions for group sessions during which anonymous or outside papers are being revised and edited by the entire class. This is the time to point out mistakes, problems, weak spots, and to invite student critics to do the same.

5. Remember that the writer owns the piece. You may see real potential in a story and feel frustrated to see that potential go undeveloped. Wouldn't it be wonderful if we found out what happened after Aunt Alice moved to Boring or why Ralph shot himself or whether Wilbur ever made the team? If you really want to find out what happens, write your own version of the unfinished story. Then it will be yours and you can do what you want with it.

6. Make student writers responsible for their own revising and editing. You are not an editor-on-call. You are responsible for teaching students revising and editing skills; you are not responsible for doing the revising and editing yourself.

Some imperfect papers are going to slip through. Let them. If you try to fix them, you'll always feel overwhelmed and resentful, and students will continue to feel incompetent and indifferent. This situation will never get better until you put the responsibility where it belongs: with the students.

7. Teach your students to use reference books to get the specific information that they need for revising and editing. Don't feel that you have to make them proficient in this skill within one term or even within one year. For some, just knowing what kinds of information are in such books will be a major step forward. Most people, English teachers included, do not know all the rules governing English grammar and punctuation. This is why reference books are invaluable for the serious editor. Of course, learning to use them well takes time, but it's amazing how often teachers who say this skill is beyond their students will ask these same students to memorize dozens of rules that have no meaning out of context.

8. Form peer support groups early in the writing process. Writers need the support of their colleagues when their ideas are first taking shape just as much as they do later on when they are preparing to revise their papers. Further, colleagues who are in on this process from the beginning provide better help in revision.

9. Don't give up conferencing just because you think you can't fit it into your schedule. Consider it as an alternative to (at least some) regular class sessions. For many students, the time will be better spent, and you'll have the hours you need to give each student individual attention.

Teach students to confer with one another. What students need is not so much to be able to confer with you *personally* (though this is hard for all of us to accept) as to have a good listener who will hear what *they* have to say about their own writing.

10. Don't grade everything that the students produce. Let the student writers choose which pieces will be graded. Consider that they may wish to leave a piece for a time and then return to it. This is what professional writers do. It's better for the piece and better for the writer. Don't publish everything, either. Think how it would be if you had to send *everything* you wrote to a publisher. How inhibiting. How dull. You don't have to finish what you start. If it's no good, throw it away.

11. Make revision the heart of the writing process. Prewriting is important, but it should never be allowed to usurp most of the in-class time devoted to writing. We need to put some balance back in the process by allotting time for drafting, reviewing, analyzing and assessing, and revising.

12. Be a writer. Write at home and bring your text into class to share with your students. Write with your students in class. Work at getting something published outside the classroom, and share your experiences —at least some of them. Keep a journal. It will give you a revealing sense of your own growth as a writer.

You will surprise yourself with how much you have to say and with what fine teaching comes out of sharing what you learn. You will also discover that students *can* write after all, and you will look forward to reading what they have to say.

APPENDIX———

PLACES THAT PUBLISH STUDENT WRITING

YOUNG AUTHOR MARKETS

This is a list of where you can publish your creative writing. Keep this list handy. It will help you locate a publisher for your students' work.

Contests and Publications Open to Young Writers

CONTESTS

National Achievement in Writing Awards (National Council of Teachers of English, 1111 Kenyon Road, Urbana, IL 61801). Essay-writing awards given to senior high-school students.

The Cricket Magazine for Children (Cricket League, Box 100, LaSalle, IL 61301). Story-writing contests for age thirteen and under.

Elias Leiberman Student Poetry Award (Poetry Society of America, 15 Gramercy Park, New York, NY 10003). Awards of $100 given high-school students.

Guideposts Magazine Youth Writing Contest (Guideposts Associates, Inc., 747 Third Avenue, New York, NY 10017). For high-school juniors and seniors. Scholarships of $1,000–$4,000 given for best personal-experience stories.

Starfire Writing and Art Contest (Chris Weber, editor, Atkinson School, 5800 SE Division, Portland, OR 97206). Nonfiction stories, fourth through eighth grades, and art, first through twelfth grades, published yearly in *Treasures*.

PUBLICATIONS

Alive for Young Teens (Christian Board of Publication, Box 179, St. Louis, MO 63166). Publishes fiction, nonfiction, poetry, puzzles, riddles, tongue-twisters, daffy-nitions by twelve- to fifteen-year-olds.

All American High School Magazine (Box 254800, Sacramento, CA 95865). Publishes fiction by high-school students.

Boy's Life Magazine (1325 Walnut Hill Land, Irving, TX 75062). Readers' page for interesting ideas and a column on hobby projects.

Christian Living for Senior Highs (David C. Cook Publishing Company, 850 N. Grove, Elgin, IL 60120). Encourages submission of fiction and nonfiction for teenagers.

Highwire Magazine, National Student Magazine (Community Publishing Services, Box 948, 217 Jackson Street, Lowell, MA 01853). Publishes fiction, nonfiction, and fillers for high-school students.

Jack and Jill (Box 567, Indianapolis, IN 46206). Stories, poems, riddles, and jokes written by children are considered.

Just About Me (JAM) (Ensio Industries, 247 Marlee Avenue, Suite 206, Toronto, Ontario, Canada M6B 4B8). A magazine for girls; accepts fiction and poetry from girls ages twelve to nineteen.

McGuffey Writer (400A McGuffey Hall, Miami University, Oxford, OH 45056). Magazine of short stories, essays, poetry, illustrations, and cartoons. Write for information and publication guidelines.

Merlyn's Pen (National Magazine for Student Writing, Box 716, East Greenwich, RI 02818). Magazine of short stories, essays, movie scripts, drawings, music and book reviews. Write for information and publication guidelines.

Probe (Baptist Brotherhood Commission, 1548 Poplar Avenue, Memphis TN 38104). Wants personal experience stories by teenage boys ages twelve to seventeen.

Purple Cow: Atlanta's Magazine for Kids (110 E. Andrews Drive NW, Atlanta, GA 30305). Publishes fiction and fillers for twelve- to eighteen-year-olds.

Ranger Rick (1412 16th Street NW, Washington, DC 20036). Includes fiction, nonfiction, and puzzles for children on nature/ecology theme.

Seventeen (850 Third Avenue, New York, NY 10022). Publishes nonfiction, fiction, poetry by teenagers; also includes a column written by teenagers, "Free for All," with profiles, essays, exposés, reportage, book reviews, and puzzles.

Student Showcase (Oregon Association of Talented and Gifted, Box 1703, Beaverton, OR 97075). Magazine for any student writing or art work.

The Sunshine News (Canada Sunshine Publishing, Ltd., 465 King Street East #14A, Toronto, Ontario, Canada M5A 1L6). A "participation magazine" for high-school students.

Young Ambassador (Good News Broadcasting Association, Inc., Box 82808, Lincoln, NE 68501). Wants short fillers from twelve- to sixteen-year-olds.

Young Author's Magazine (Box 6294, Lincoln, NB 68506). Publishes short stories, articles, interviews, essays, poems, one-act plays. Write for information and publication guidelines.

Children's House/Children's World
Children's House, Inc.
Box 111, Caldwell, NJ 07006

Child's Play
Childs Play Information Centre
31 Tooley Street
London SE1, England

Childworld
Christian Children's Fund
Development Office
Box 26511
Richmond, VA 23261

Christian Home
Upper Room
1908 Grand Avenue
Nashville, TN 37212

Creative Children and Adults' Quarterly
National Association for
Creative Children and Adults
8080 Spring Valley Drive
Cincinnati, OH 45236

Family Journal
Box 815
Battlehorn, UT 05301

G/C/T
GCT Publishing Company
Box 66654
Mobile, AL 36660

Gifted Child Quarterly
160 Monroe Drive
Williamsville, NY 14221

Growing Up Whole
Camar Publications
125, Station G
Calgary, ALB T3A 2G1
Canada

Guiding
Girl Guides Association
17-19 Buckingham Palace Road
London SW1, England

High/Low Report
Riverhouse Publications
20 Waterside Plaza
New York, NY 10010

National 4-H News
National 4-H Council
7100 Connecticut Avenue
Chevy Chase, MD 20815

REFERENCES

Anderson, Richard C., et al. 1985. *Becoming a Nation of Readers*. Washington, D.C.: U.S. Department of Education.

Atwell, Nancie. 1987. *In the Middle: Writing, Reading and Learning with Adolescents*. Portsmouth, NH: Boynton/Cook Publishers.

_____. 1985. "Writing and Reading from the Inside Out." In *Breaking Ground: Teachers Relate Reading and Writing in the Elementary School*. Edited by Jane Hansen, Thomas Newkirk, and Donald Graves. Portsmouth, NH: Heinemann Educational Books.

Bleich, David. 1975. *Readings and Feelings*. Urbana, IL: National Council of Teachers of English.

Calkins, Lucy McCormick. 1986. *The Art of Teaching Writing*. Portsmouth, NH: Heinemann Educational Books.

Chew, Charles. 1985. "Instruction Can Link Reading and Writing." In *Breaking Ground: Teachers Relate Reading and Writing in the Elementary School*. Edited by Jane Hansen, Thomas Newkirk, and Donald Graves. Portsmouth, NH: Heinemann Educational Books.

Diederich, Paul B. 1974. *Measuring Growth in English*. Urbana, IL: National Council of Teachers of English.

DuBois, P. H. 1970. *A History of Psychological Testing*. Boston: Allyn & Bacon.

Elbow, Peter. 1987. *Embracing Contraries*. New York: Oxford University Press.

_____. 1973. *Writing Without Teachers*. New York: Oxford University Press.

Graves, Donald H. 1986. In *Breaking Ground: Teachers Relate Reading and Writing in the Elementary School*. Portsmouth, NH: Heinemann Educational Books.

_____. 1983. *Writing: Teachers and Children at Work*. Portsmouth, NH: Heinemann Educational Books.

_____, and Virginia Stuart. 1985. *Write from the Start: Tapping Your Child's Natural Writing Ability*. New York: NAL Penguin.

Hairston, Maxine. 1986. "On Not Being a Composition Slave." In *Training the New Teacher of College Composition*. Edited by Charles W. Bridges. Urbana, IL.: National Council of Teachers of English.

Hansen, Jane. 1985. "Skills." In *Breaking Ground: Teachers Relate Reading and Writing in the Elementary School*. Portsmouth, NH: Heinemann Educational Books.

Hillocks, George, Jr. 1986. *Research on Written Composition: New Directions for Teaching.* Urbana, IL: ERIC Clearinghouse on Reading and Communications Skills.

Langer, Judith A., and Arthur N. Applebee. 1987. *How Writing Shapes Thinking.* Urbana, IL : National Council of Teachers of English.

McCrum, Robert, William Cran, and Robert McNeil. 1986. *The Story of English.* New York: Viking Penguin.

Moffett, James. 1983. "Reading and Writing." In *Composing and Comprehending.* Edited by Julie M. Jensen. Urbana, IL : ERIC Clearinghouse on Reading and Communication Skills.

Mohr, Marian M. 1984. *Revision: The Rhythm of Meaning.* Upper Montclair, NJ: Boynton/Cook Publishers.

Murray, Donald. 1985. *A Writer Teaches Writing.* 2nd ed. Boston: Houghton Mifflin.

————. 1984. *Write to Learn.* New York: Holt, Rinehart & Winston.

Perl, Sondra, and Nancy Wilson. 1986. *Through Teachers' Eyes: Portraits of Writing Teachers at Work.* Portsmouth, NH : Heinemann Educational Books.

Pooley, Robert C. 1974. *The Teaching of English Usage,* 2nd ed. Urbana, IL: National Council of Teachers of English.

Rouse, John. 1978. *The Completed Gesture: Myth, Character and Education.* New Jersey: Skyline Books.

Smith, Frank. 1984. "Reading Like a Writer." In *Composing and Comprehending.* Edited by Julie M. Jensen. Urbana, IL : ERIC Clearinghouse on Reading and Communication Skills.

Tate, Gary. 1981. "The Basics in the 80s." In *Education in the 80s: English.* Edited by R. Baird Shuman. Washington, D.C.: National Education Association.

Trelease, Jim. 1985. *The Read-Aloud Handbook.* New York: Viking Penguin.

Weaver, Constance. 1979. *Grammar for Teachers: Perspectives and Definitions.* Urbana, IL : National Council of Teachers of English.

Welty, Eudora. 1983. *One Writer's Beginnings.* New York: Warner Books.

Ziegler, Alan. 1981. *The Writing Workshop.* Vol. 1. New York: Teachers and Writers Collaborative.

INDEX